AF517855

Bubble

A Study of Scam, Scandal and Corruption in Indian Stock Market

Madhusudan Karmakar

2024

Regency Publications

A Division of

Astral International Pvt. Ltd.

New Delhi – 110 002

© 2024, AUTHOR
ISBN: 978-81-8603-095-0 (HB)

Disclaimer:

Every possible effort has been made to ensure that the information contained in this book is accurate at the time of going to press, and the publisher and author cannot accept responsibility for any errors or omissions, however caused. No responsibility for loss or damage occasioned to any person acting, or refraining from action, as a result of the material in this publication can be accepted by the editor, the publisher or the author. The Publisher is not associated with any product or vendor mentioned in the book. The contents of this work are intended to further general scientific research, understanding and discussion only. Readers should consult with a specialist where appropriate.

Every effort has been made to trace the owners of copyright material used in this book, if any. The author and the publisher will be grateful for any omission brought to their notice for acknowledgment in the future editions of the book.

All Rights reserved under International Copyright Conventions. No part of this publication may be reproduced, stored in a retrieval system, or transmitted in any form or by any means, electronic, mechanical, photocopying, recording or otherwise without the prior written consent of the publisher and the copyright owner.

Published by : **Regency Publications**
A Division of
Astral International Pvt. Ltd.
– ISO 9001:2015 Certified Company –
4736/23, Ansari Road, Darya Ganj
New Delhi-110 002
Ph. 011A43549197, 23278134
E-mail: info@astralint.com
Website: www.astralint.com

PREFACE

Probably at no time since independence, has there been so much enthusiasm in Indian stock market as it was found in the share mania of eighties. After a prolonged gap of many years the stock market once again became the subject of widespread interest among investors, market authorities, and the government; and their joint endeavour made a "new era" of rising stock price specially at the beginning of 90s.

During the hey-days of unprecedented share market boom, the carefree investors were thrilled with the fabulous rates of return, the government was jubilant with incredible fund mobilising capacity of the market, and the market authorities were proud with the changing image and increasing importance of stock market in the national economy. Though there was enough indication, in those days, that the market was behaving irrationally, it was extremely volatile and it's future course of movement was simply unpredictable, they preferred to brush aside all these danger signals temporarily. But the cost of ignoring the tell-tale signs and portents of disasters in the market was strongly felt after unearthing of everlargest financial scandal in the history of India, popularly known as "Security Scam". It exposed how different government controlled organisations along with many other existing structural as well as operational imperfections of capital market contributed to violent fluctuation in share prices. It shattered the confidence of investors on capital and money markets and the functioning of these markets was thrown in disarray. The fate of new economic policy, the very foundation on which the boom was based, suffered a severe setback. The whole episode unveiled a few naked truths and provoked endless debate on inadequacy and need for capital market reforms of our country.

At the height of the market buoyancy the social conversation was, in fact, dominated by the stock market and it can hardly escape the attention of any student of financial economics like me. The incidence of sky-rocketing high price in boom market followed by the precipitous price drops in post boom period made me curious about the functioning of the stock market and ultimately inspired me to conduct an extensive study in this area. After the market debacle, the much talked about "meltdown" raised a number of questions such as—What factors were responsible for unbelievable rise and dramatic fall in share prices? What were the roles of irrational waves of optimism and pessimism in the whole episode? Why should we care about excessive fluctuation of share prices? What are the implications of irrational behaviour of market for public policy? What are the different steps taken so far to liberalise Indian financial system? Are the steps taken sufficient to improve the efficiency of the market? What is the impact of liberalisation on stock market behaviour? To what extent does the present behaviour of the market impair the development process of our economy? Can we depend on stock market for fair pricing thereby efficient allocation of resources? Is there any necessity to replace it, where possible, by other institutions that provide a more sober and hence more accurate measure of value? Should the government intervene in the operation of the market to protect the interest of investors? The present study entitled *"Bubble: A Study of Scam, Scandal and Corruption in Indian Stock Market"*, is a modest attempt to answer the above questions. The study would also focus on the associated social cost and suggest remedies for capital market on whose performance the success of new economic policy largely depends.

The present work is a revised version of my Ph.D. thesis which was submitted to the University of North Bengal. In completing the book I have incurred immense debts: My greatest gratitude is to Dr. M.K. Roy, Reader in Commerce, NBU, who was my Ph.D. supervisor and has always been a source of inspiration. The study has been enriched by the critical comments and valuable suggestions made by

Dr. R.N. Bhattacharyya, Professor in Economics, Kalyani University, and Dr. I. Roy, Lecturer in Commerce, NBU. I sincerely thank Dr. A.K. Roy, Reader in Commerce, NBU, for his courteous help in preparing the computer programmes that were needed for data processing in the study.

I am also thankful to the officers and staff of North Bengal University Library, National Library, Calcutta, and Bidhan Chandra Memorial Library of IIM, Calcutta for making available all the library facilities needed for the work.

I take this opportunity to record the help and encouragement that I have received from my colleagues and friends, especially Dr. S. Nag of Assam University, Silchar in getting the study revised.

Finally, I record my deep sense of gratitude to my parents who have been a continuous source of inspiration in getting the study completed.

1st September, 1997 **Madhusudan Karmakar**
Assam University

CONTENTS

Preface	iii
List of Tables	ix
List of Figures	xi
***Chapter One*: Introduction**	1
***Chapter Two*: Some Methodological Issues**	23
***Chapter Three*: Measurement of Stock Price Volatility**	41
***Chapter Four*: Volatility and Market Efficiency**	66
***Chapter Five*: Summing Up and Policy Implications**	81
Appendices	111
Select Bibliography	122
Index	130

LIST OF TABLES

2.1. Definition of Principal Symbols 37
3.1. Decadewise Analysis of Volatility of Monthly Return 44
3.2. Top 10 Volatile Years 45
3.3. Mean and Standard Deviation of Daily Return by Decade, May 1961 to December 1992 47
3.4. 25 Highest Volatile Months 50
3.5. Number of Changes in Daily Prices in Excess of Plus or Minus 2.34134 per cent, May 1961–December 1992 55
3.6. Daily Price Changes in Excess of Plus or Minus 3 per cent 1961–1992 56
3.7. Associated Events Released in the Vicinity of Price Swings in Excess of Plus or Minus 3 per cent During the Period 1985–1992 58
4.1. Sample Statistics for Price and Dividend Series 70
4.2. Sample Statistics for Revised Detrended Price and Dividend Series (1968–1991) 74
5.1. Key Indicators of the Growth Pattern of Indian Stock Market, Pre and Post Liberalisation Period 94
5.2. Volatility of Monthly Return: Pre and Post Liberalisation Period 95
5.3 Capital Issues, Quarterly Review of 1992 98

LIST OF FIGURES

2.1. Alternative Estimators of Volatility, Average Daily Share Price of Top 20 Companies by Turnover (January–December 1990) 27
3.1. Yearly Standard Deviation of Monthly Return 43
3.2. Monthly % Standard Deviation of Daily Return 49
3.3. Daily Change > 2 Per Cent Threshold 53
3.4. Daily Change > 1 Per Cent Threshold 54
3.5. Monthly % SD of Normal Return 62
4.1. Price (p) Volatility and Ex post Rational Price (p^*) Variability 69
4.2. Alternative Measures of Ex post Rational Price Series (p_t^*) 71
4.3. Extent of Price Variation Explained by σ (d) 72
4.4. Demand Curves with Fixed Supply 75
4.5. Changes in Equilibrium 75
4.6. Demand Curves of Alternative Approach 77

CHAPTER I

INTRODUCTION

Economists' endeavour to explore the mystery of asset price movement may be traced back to the beginning of the present century (Bachelier, 1900). After a prolonged gap of over half a century, the finance literature witnessed a resurgence of interest among scholars on asset market behaviour (Osborne, 1962; Mandelbrot, 1963; Sharpe, 1964; Samuelson, 1965; Lintner, 1965). Summarising all these early ventures, Fama (1970) ultimately developed a comprehensive theoretical framework to explain share price behaviour—popularly known as Efficient Market Hypothesis. The theory which is often acclaimed as the best established fact in all of social sciences (Jensen, 1978), shattered many of our long cherished belief about market behaviour. Ultimately collective effort of modern finance's pioneers was honoured by the Nobel Committee in Economics when it awarded its 1990 prize to Harry Morkowitz, Merton Miller and William Sharpe.

How does the efficient market behave? Rational Expectation theory holds that a stock's current market value tends to converge to the discounted present value of the rationally expected dividend stream (Smith, Suchanek and Williams, 1988). If this theory holds good, the share price would always be in equilibrium. Price may, of course, deviate temporarily from the 'fair' value due to the presence of irrational investors. Economists, however, feel safe to ignore the role of "noise" traders[1] in their discussion on asset price formation. They argue that irrational investors are met in the market by rational arbitrageurs, who trade against them and in the process drive prices close to fundamental values (Friedman, 1953 and Fama, 1965), leaving no further scope of 'poaching'

(Zeckhauser, Patel and Hendricks, 1991). Equilibrium price, of course, will shift instantly and constantly in response to new information that changes the investors' expectation. In a market with instantaneous price adjustment, the movement of price is directly related to the rate of arrival of new information. Hence, price volatility simply equals information volatility (Ross, 1989).

The truly efficient market in the strict sense of the term, is an ideal institution that every society dreams of. An obvious reason is that the more quickly and accurately prices reflect new information, the more efficient would be the pricing of securities and thereby the allocation of resources. The situation would no doubt yield maximum benefit for the welfare of the society. If asset prices do not reflect fundamentals well, then the confidence of economists in the efficiency of market allocations of investment resources is, to say the least, weakened (Stiglitz, 1990).

Are financial markets efficient? Do their participants behave rationally? Does this paradigm capture most financial market behaviour? These questions still remain open despite decades of effort by economists and numerous claims that the issues have been resolved.

Surprisingly the pursuit of academic researchers to develop an alternative explanation of investors' behaviour appears to have more or less died out in the 1950's at about the time when the rational expectation theory was born. The world market crash of 1987 proved that market decision makers are not as rational as the rational expectation theorists believe (Shiller, 1987; Shiller and Pound, 1988; Shiller, Kon-Ya and Tsutsui, 1989). If this conjecture is correct, the simple and elegant model of the economists, whatever appealing it might be, proves to be inadequate to describe how the economic actors really behave in the market to form their expectation. It inspired academics once again to search for an alternative explanation of investors' behaviour based on market psychology, the references of which are available in the "Bubble"[2] literature (West, 1988; Stiglitz, 1990; Shleifer and Summers, 1990; Garber, 1990; Shiller, 1990; Zeckhauser, Patel, and Hendricks, 1991). The jargons which are extensively used in the "Bubble" literature but conspicuously absent in the economists' writings, such as "panic", "crash", "financial crisis", "crowd behaviour", "social learnings", "expert and reliance effect", "status quo bias" etc., immediately evoke images of frenzied and probably irrational speculative activities. These events hint that the rationality paradigm may not be universally applicable.

A Detour through History: A Study of Bubble Burst Phenomeon

In this section we would take a brief detour through history of Indian stock market so as to have glimpse of idea, of course, not based on hard facts—how investors really behave in asset market that results movement in share prices. Our trip will not be that of an economic historian as we are not looking for specific dates or facts *per se*; instead we are trying to gain an insight into the event that results in abrupt changes in the demand for an asset and thereby its prices.

Share Mania of 1860–65

The American Civil War broke out in 1860–61. It was in fact a blessing for Indian Cotton growers. The War eventuated unbelievable demand for Indian Cotton by Lancashire mills that led to a boom in cotton prices. Cotton traders in India amassed vast fortune and with the wealth they secured at that time, numerous mushroom companies were started, almost for every imaginable purpose. A part of the wealth also found its way in the stock market, that along with temporal prosperity gave birth to the first-ever speculative fever of Indian stock market at its infancy.

Excessive speculation became hectic and the share prices danced further and further away from all the benchmarks of fundamental values. The frenzy that seized the people at large was indescribable. The people only woke up when the War came to an end. The boom collapsed, the premiums vanished, prices dropped to a discount and the investing public was left holding a huge mass of unsaleable paper. "The nadir of depression was reached on 1 July 1865, popularly known as the 'Black Friday', when hundreds of time bargains matured which no one was in a position to fulfil" (Gupta, 1972).

This scanty description of investor behaviour is difficult to explain by economic model. It seems that the unusual price rise ensued from over-optimism and the abnormal price drop stemmed from panic. More simply, during a bull market, investors could become greedy and act as risk lovers, while during a bear market they could be fearful and risk averse.

A Replica of Old Story

Following the share mania of 1860–65, Indian stock market remained almost stable throughout the next fifty years. Cloud of panic and pessimism following a series of bank failures in 1914 (Goldsmith, 1983), was abruptly blown away by the magical effect of First World War. In the domestic market, thanks to the War, there was cessation of foreign competition and in the foreign market new demand was created for Indian product. To satisfy unprecedented demand with prevailing production capacity, factories and workshops in India worked round the clock to reap fabulous profit. Tremendous rise in profit was followed by declaration to unbelievable dividends by some industries to its shareholders.

With exceptionally strong fundamentals,[3] optimism engulfed the stock market. New bubble came enticing both professional and amateur investors into the boiling market with a view to make their fortune. The temporal prosperity was in fact war sponsored (Gadgil, 1929), but the crazy investors had an expectation of the continuation of the prevailing heydays. They even did not care to pay for some select shares a price equivalent to a deluxe motor car. For all practical purposes most shares were beyond the reach of many investors having limited funds to spare. It led them to think in terms of co-operative investment—a concept that has a close familiarity with the present day mutual fund. As public appetite whetted, rampant speculative activities started and soon market was degenerated into an arena of gamble. Thus, share price index started mounting up and it shot up to the sky when it reached 295 in 1921 (1914=100) (Gupta, 1972). Madness of investors equally infected primary market.

Before the issue of the script, shares were often traded at a premium. Market value of share capital of many newly established companies doubled before even the first sod was turned.[4]

Eventually the boom burst in October 1921, a replay of 1860–65 drop and thereafter a slump set in.[5] Share prices touched to the bottom and the price index (1914=100) plunged downwards from 295 in 1921 to 169 in 1923 (Gupta, 1972). It appears when the crowd began to realize the excess of the boom there was scramble to escape resulting in panic which carried values far below the point from which the mania started.

Drama Replayed

Hardly twenty years after the First World War boom,[6] amidst intense struggle for freedom and bloody Second World War, paradoxically Indian economy took a curious turn for growth and prosperity. Though share price started booming right from the beginning of the devastating war that broke out on 3rd September 1939, the real frenzy began when the Allies were winning. India was fully mobilized as a supply base that resulted in hectic business activity all around. Enthusiasm and confidence engulfed the stock market too. Price rose steadily upto September 1945, then there was simply a fantastic increase in share prices. The speculative elements of other trades were also attracted to the stock market resulting share price index (1927–28=100) to shot up almost vertically from 277.2 in September 1945 to 396.3 in June 1946 and hit the top at 455.2 in August 1946 (Gupta, 1972). Share price indices of many industries almost doubled and it appeared as if sky is the limit.

War-stimulated-demand started disappearing quickly after the restoration of peace and the most delightful dream eventually ended. The crisis that followed was serious both in Calcutta and Bombay where a large number of mushroom banks that had been making liberal advances on shares came to grief and had to close their doors. Share prices crashed like a house of cards and the index plunged down from 452.2 in August to 342 in December, 1946 thus recording an alpine fall of more than 100 points in three months. The fall continued till it reached at its bottom at 131.1 in July 1949 (Gupta, 1972). Loss of faith on share market was total, membership of stock market declined dramatically, a number of markets that emerged during the War either went into liquidation or merged with bigger one.

It appears, both in rising and falling markets the notions of intrinsic worth[7] or fairness played insignificant role in the investors' buy or sell decision. The degree of risk perceived was clearly lowest in the boom markets. Rising prices seemed to have dampened fears, and that fuelled the boom. Similarly falling price created panic, and investors overestimated the associated risk. Since one's willingness to pay for an asset depends in part on the perceived degree of risk associated with it, the underestimation and overestimation of risk caused the irrational price movements in boom as well as slump periods (Case and Shiller, 1988).

The Common Characteristics

Though timing and participants differ, there are surprisingly some common characteristics among all the speculative episodes. One such feature is that every boom starts in response to strong fundamentals. When price increases, "trend chasing" investors[8] following the strategy of "riding the winners" (Zeckhauser, Patel and Hendricks, 1991), accelerate the rise in price-which is often described as "price-to-price channel" impact (Shiller, 1987). The tendency to look beyond the simple fact of increasing values to the reasons on which it depends greatly diminishes (Galbraith, 1961), ultimately the index number hits the top.

Following the rules of the market, eclipse follows illumination, panicky investors start deserting market in 'herds' and prices continue to plummet. In fact, people react to price changes themselves, so that price drop feeds on itself in a vicious circle (Shiller, 1987), and eventually index number touches the bottom.

It appears that rationality becomes the first victim in each bubble-burst phenomenon. Investors in fact care little about 'fair' or 'intrinsic' value of share and their opinion is virtually guided by the whims of the moment. After each boom followed by a slump, people start soul searching but learn little and burn their fingers repeatedly.

Does History Repeat Itself?

Bidding farewell to "control regime", Indian economy was gradually entering into an era of liberalisation from early eighties. The opening up of the Indian economy as a result of this measure[9] promised an unprecedented growth and prosperity for the private corporate sector. Anticipating good tidings for the private sector, the stock market started booming. The buoyancy of the market can easily be guessed in terms of funds raised from the market, daily turnover of the stock exchanges, expansion of investors population, rate of market capitalisation, the increase in the number of stock exchange and listed companies etc.[10]

Together with all these welcome developments, stock market started witnessing a steady rise in share prices since the beginning of the decade 80s. The market buoyancy continued over the decade with a few setback and gained momentum since 1990 with the Bombay Stock Exchange Sensitive Index (Sensex) rose from 781.1 in March 1990 to 1270 in April 1992 (1978–79 = 100). But what happened after the Union Budget of 1992–93, was a miracle in the Indian capital market. Share prices shot up almost vertically attracting, like months to a candle, many new persons from all walks of life, who indulged in share trading tempted by the ambition to make a fortune within the twinkling of an eye. The sensex which stood at 1764 in September 1991, jumped to 3333.2 in March 1992 and finally hit the top at 4387.8 in April 1992, thus recording a meteoric rise of 1569 points in a short span of six months and that of 1054 points in less than a month. The spiraling price index aroused an instinctive feeling among the investors that the market is behaving irrationally, it is extremely volatile and its future course of action is simply unpredictable.[11]

Of course, higher volatility might not be an unmixed curse when it represents the faster incorporation of new information into price. Thus during the days of price rise there was an attempt by academics as well as professionals[12] to justify present movement in terms of arrival of information. It was argued, large scale participation of smart money mangers, introduction of venture capital, use of computer, development of communication system, increased awareness of individual investors, flow of information regarding fundamental factors altogether contributed in the capacities of the market to learn about and to react to information very quickly. Thus the rate at which price changes in response to information has also increased in recent period. This is an essential feature of efficient market, a cherised belief of some of financial economists about stock market behaviour (Fama, 1970).

This academic approach of market behaviour was, however, shattered after unearthing of ever-largest financial scandal in the history of India, popularly known as "security scam". The whole episode of scam unveiled the fact that collosal amount of funds was being illegally diverted from banking sector to finance the speculative activities in the stock market. When the scandal was exposed, the government responded harshly, flow of excess money stopped and panicky investors started deserting stock market *en masse*. An almost inevitable reaction set in and the crowd became as extreme in its panic as it had been in its euphoria.

With the public in the throes of a panic, the stock continued to plummet. The sensex which stood at 4387.8 in April 1992 descended sharply to 3560.7 in May 1992, recording an alpine fall of 827 points within a month and its downward journey continued thereafter. In less than two months following the discovery of scam, market value of shares vanished to the tune of Rs. 1,00,000 crores. The fate of new economic policy, the very foundation on which the boom was based, suffered a big jolt, and the functioning of market was thrown in disarray. The whole episode unveiled a few naked truths and provoked endless debate on inadequacy and need for capital market reform of our country. The crisis evoked public clamour for an enquiry into the financial scandal and accordingly a large number of agencies[13] was directed by the government to investigate various aspects of the scam.

Most interestingly there was a shift in the investors' opinion. They started believing that the market debacle specially after the scam, makes a mockery of academic claim that stock market is efficient. Because, the present "meltdown" is difficult to explain by the notion of market rationality conceived by efficient market theorists.

Research Questions

In view of the above conflicting assertions regarding the causes of present share price movements, it requires to investigate—Does the current share market boom and burst replicate old experiences? Or does it reflect its own unique feature? To answer these questions, of course, we have to take resort to objective analysis based on hard facts, giving up subjective evaluation tried so far to explain earlier speculative episodes. Thus the issues directly related to the questions raised above are—what is the average level of volatility of Indian stock market? Has it increased in the current period? Is it really alarming at least in historical perspective? All these research questions would help us to investigate the validity of investors belief about increased volatility in the recent time. Further issues that are closely associated with the explanation of market volatility are—What causes sudden and often dramatic and sustained price movements? Can the price movement be explained by fundamental economic factors? If not, what are the other variables that influence share prices? The answers of the above nagging questions would help us to examine whether history repeats itself or market proves to have been efficient in recent period.

Curiously, whole debate on the present state of share price movement, its plausible explanations and development implications, still now, is simply based on general observation of market behaviour that lacks adequate rigour. Strangely enough, there has not been any modest attempt to measure the stock price volatility in Indian market, neither had there been any serious investigation to justify the price movement in a logical way. Present study aims to put the gamut of issues into a proper perspective, to study policy implications of the ongoing debate.

Scope of the Study

To seek appropriate answers to the questions raised above, it becomes imperative to test at least following two hypotheses:

(a) Current (1981–92) share price movement has suppressed all previous records.
It requires measurement of share price fluctuation on an objective basis and to compare the current (1981–92) state of volatility with that of historical standard (1935–92). and,

(b) Present share price movement can be explained by Efficient Market Paradigm.

It needs to prove that only objective variables influenced share price movement.

In fact present study aims to measure and provide a reasonable explanation of share price movements of Indian stock market. These issues are directly or indirectly related to some major policy implications such as:

- Why should we care about excessive fluctuation of share prices?
- What are the implications of irrational behaviour of market for public policy?
- What are the different steps taken so far to liberalise Indian financial system?
- Are the steps taken sufficient to improve the efficiency of the market?
- What is the impact of financial liberalisation on the share price fluctuations?
- To what extent does the present behaviour of stock market impair the development process of our economy?
- Would it be appropriate to ban forward trading to get rid of the ills of overspeculation?
- What role should the government controlled financial institutions play in the stock market?
- Are the mechanisms to control speculative activities such as imposition of margin money, transfer of shares from specified to cash list, volume restriction etc. truly effective?

- What role should the Security and Exchange Board of India (SEBI) play for smooth functioning of the market?
- Is there any need to change the organisational structure of the stock market to improve its efficiency?
- Is there any need for government intervention in the operation of the market to protect the interest of general investors?

The study, we believe, would help us to grasp pitfalls and suggest remedies for capital market on whose performance success of new economic policy largely depends.

Review of Literature

After publication of Fama's celebrated article on "Efficient Capital markets" in 1970, it became fashionable for the academics to assume that stock price tends to reflect the fundamental value. This presumption was seriously challenged by Shiller in 1981, and since the publication of a paper by Blanchard and Waston in 1982, there has been a search for speculative bubbles of a rational nature. The ongoing debate gave birth to vast literature but the controversy around the explanation of price movement still remains unresolved. The literature is now so voluminous that a full review is in fact impossible. Instead, we would only concentrate on the works which are directly related to our studies i.e., the literature concerning the measurement of stock price volatility and those directed to provide plausible explanations behind the price movement.

Different scholars have examined a number of estimators ranging from traditional standard deviation to extreme value methods for the measurement of share price movement. Parkinson (1980) was first to introduce the high-low estimator, otherwise known as extreme value method which is far superior to the traditional measure based on close-to-close standard deviation. It is only after Parkinson (1980), several improved methods of higher efficiency have been proposed for estimating the volatility parameter by Garman & Klass (1980), Beckers (1981), (1983), Cox and Rubinstein (1985), and Kunitomo (1992). All these writings nicely summed up different models of volatility measurement before proposing an alternative method. Their proposed measures, however, owe much to the idea first developed by Parkinson, who may be considered as one of the most celebrated researchers in this area. While the above methods for estimating volatility parameter are helpful to serve the academic evidence on stock market fluctuation, Kritzman (1991) offers an excellent discussion for practitioners of what they need to know about estimating volatility.

Though the effort to develop scientific approach to estimate market volatility started long ago, the endeavour to measure volatility objectively applying the above tools received considerable attention in the finance literature over the last few years. The issue in true sense has become loudest especially since the October 19, 1987 stock market crash. The precipitous price drop led regulators, policy makers and the investors to worry whether price volatility is increasing and thus stimulated researchers for the first time to measure stock price volatility in quantitative terms. In this attempt, many researchers in the west have done praiseworthy works, notably, Jones and Wilson (1989), Harries (1989), Schwert (1990). All of them simply measured stock price volatility in historical perspective ignoring the reasons behind this price movement. Another relevant study which deserves special mention is Schwert (1989). The researcher in his study not only measured stock volatility but also analysed related macro economic variables and tried to associate them with stock price movement.

To address the question what causes stock price movement, the finance literature provides divergent views of economists. Though approaches of researchers differ, all the studies, however, may be conveniently categorized into two broad groups. Some trace the price movement back to the fundamental economic factors while others present a great deal of evidences suggesting that market psychology is the dominant cause of price movement.

Much of the empirical literature on security prices have been directed at the fundamental economic factors to explain day-to-day movement in price. Samuelson (1965) and Mandlebrot (1966) for the first time, argued that 'random' price movements were consistent with a market in which all participants had equal access to information. In such a market, defined to be 'fair market', security price tends to reflect the 'true' or 'fair' value. The extremely quoted study in this area is Fama (1970) who presents an excellent review of empirical and theoretical literature under the rubric of Efficient Market Hypothesis. The Hypothesis together with the empirical tests (Cootner, 1962; Fama, 1965; Fama and Blume, 1966; Niederhoffer and Osborne, 1966; Ball and Brown, 1968) establishing its validity, is considered to be one of the most important achievements in finance theory during the 1970s. Although there were serious questions about the foundations upon which the new theory was built, there was nothing better to give a more rational explanation of how the speculative prices move. As a result a number of researchers contributed to this endeavour that ultimately enriched the rational expectation theory (Fama, Fisher, Jensen, and Roll, 1969; Jensen, 1978; Boldt and Arbit, 1984; Summers, 1986).

During late seventies and early eighties, the empirical literature on market efficiency while passing through the acid test of scientific usefulness, uncovered a number of phenomena that call for theoretical explanations beyond what can be obtained by traditional rational expectation model under Efficient Market Hypothesis. The concepts of 'informational efficiency', 'arbitrage operation', 'fair value' that may be treated as the basic foundations of efficient market theory, were seriously challenged by a number of researchers and the issues which ultimately emerged were formidable.

The literature on asset markets with asymmetric information began with the development of rational expectations equilibrium models. Sanford Grossman and Joseph E. Stiglitz were the pioneers of and remain leading contributors to this subject. A series of thought provoking writings by them (Grossman, 1976; 1977; 1978 and Grossman and Stiglitz, 1976; 1980) provided a deeper analysis of what it means for security prices fully to reflect available information. They argued that as long as information is costly, capital markets can not be efficient and perfectly arbitraged—in fact "an equilibrium amount of disequilibrium" will exist in the market.

What effect do rational speculators have on asset prices? The standard answer, dating back to Friedman (1953), Baumol (1957) Telser (1959), Fama (1965), Farrell (1966), & Samuelson (1971) is that rational speculators must stabilize asset prices. The economists simply ignored the importance of the noise traders in the price formation process and argued that the rational arbitrageurs bit the noise traders and drive the prices towards fundamentals. Many researchers (Figlewski, 1979; Kyle, 1985; De Long et al., 1989; 1990a; 1990b; 1991),however, recently challenged the above hypothesis and emphasised that with the presence of risk averse arbitrageurs and 'feed-back' traders, market price strays from the theoretical value.

A widely quoted work on noise trading by Black (1986), states that stock price reflects both the 'information' that information traders trade on and the 'noise' that noise traders trade on. So thanks to informational disequilibrium and limited arbitrage that make financial market imperfect but possible. 'Fads' or 'Bubbles' thus becomes the integral part of asset price formation process. Many scholars in their attempt to prove existence of "fads" and "bubbles" in asset prices, resorted to a wide range of methodology such as statistical approach, questionnaire survey, and recourse to economic history and their findings offered serious challenge to "well research" and "elegant models" of Efficient Market Theorists.

In fact, the essence of market efficiency lost ground rapidly following the publication of Shiller's (1981a), (1981b) and LeRoy and Porter's (1981) volatility tests that substantiated—stock prices should fluctuate less than dividends. In contrast, both of them found stock market volatility to be far greater than would be predicted by a present value model where future dividends are capitalised at a constant discount rate. Kleidon (1986) and Marsh and Merton (1986), however, challenged the statistical validity of Shiller's volatility test and pointed out that excess volatility test is crucially dependent on the assumption of stationarity of dividend series. Shiller (1984) concedes this point to the critics and proposes an alternative method of detrending the data. Excess variability tests applying the detrended data once again result in a rejection of efficiency.

The Efficient Market Hypothesis crashed along with the rest of the market on October 19, 1987. Following the 'meltdown', research on popular models, using questionnaire survey methods (Shiller, 1987; Shiller and Pound, 1989; Shiller, Kon-ya, Tautsui, 1991; Case and Shiller, 1988) offers glimpses of the thought process that underlie speculative price movement. The researchers make it evident that investors psychology plays an important or even the dominating role in driving the prices from fundamental values. Thus, existence of "fads" and "bubbles" in stock market is the natural outcome. It clearly captures Keynes's (1936) notion that markets are sometimes driven by animal spirits unrelated to economic realities.

Many researchers have recoursed to economic history, in their pursuit to substantiate that asset prices do not behave in ways explainable by economic fundamentals. In a stylist analysis, Dreman (1977), takes a detour through economic history covering all the major speculative events of asset markets of the world and concludes that investors' psychology mostly influences asset prices. Van Horne (1985), accepts the possibility of bubbles and manias in financial market and refers to the Dutch tulipmania (1634–37) where a "single bulb sold for many years' salary". Referring to the tulipmania Shiller (1986) argues that asset markets are driven by capricious investors acting on the basis of fads and bubbles. In related papers, Cutler, Poterba and Summers (1989) refer to the Tulipmania, the Mississippi Bubble (1719–20) and the South Sea Bubble (1720) to exemplify how trading dynamics may affect asset prices. Finally, in the exchange rate literature, Krugman (1985) and Messe (1986) illustrate the tulipmania and the South Sea Bubble while building a case for a bubble interpretation of the movements of the dual exchange rate during the 1980s.

Obviously, all the above mentioned research works are important and interesting in their own right and any serious researcher in this area will be immensely benefited by these studies. However, in India neither any serious attempt has been made so far to measure the stock market volatility in quantitative terms, nor any effort has been found to explain the reasons for such price movements. Obviously there are some casual writings in financial papers that deserve little attention of any careful investigator. The study under consideration is an attempt to fill in this gap.

Framework of the Study

The study spans over five chapters including the present one. Chapter Two deals with the different aspects of research methodology such as data sources, the time period of the study and the different statistical tools and techniques to be used.

Chapter Three concerns with the measurement of stock price volatility in quantitative terms. Current level of volatility will be compared to the historical standard for an understanding whether it is increasing or not.

Chapter Four is mainly designed to investigate whether share price fluctuations as measured in Chapter Three can be explained by the hypothesis developed by economists or not. If our study reveals existence of bubbles in stock prices, it requires an understanding of other variables that also influence share price but have been ignored by economists.

Finally Chapter Five presents the summary of the empirical results and conclusions of the study along with the majore policy implications in the context of financial liberalisation.

NOTES

1. Noise trading is trading on noise as if it were information. People who trade on noise are willing to trade even though from an objective point of view they would be better off not trading. Perhaps they think the noise they are trading on is information. On perhaps they just like to trade. (See Black, F., 1986).
2. A bubble is simply defined as the difference between market price and market fundamental. 'The financial definition of the bubble on an asset is the difference between its price and the present discounted value of its dividends' (Tirole, Jean 1986). Kindleberger has defined bubble as 'a sharp rise in the price of an asset. . . . in a continuous process, with the initial rise generating expectations of further rises and attracting new buyers. . . . ' (Eatwell et al., 1987 Vol. I, p. 281). Another definition is that a bubble exists 'if the reason that the price is high today is only because investors believe that the selling price will be high tomorrow—when fundamental factors do not . . . . justify such a price' (Stiglitz, 1990, p. 13). The examples of bubbles which are often quoted are the South Sea Bubble in London in the 1720s and the tulipmania in seventeenth century Holland. (A brief description of some historical

bubbles is exhibited in Appendix A. For a detailed discussion see also Garber, 1990).

3. Fundamentals have been defined as 'the basic parameters defining an economy—such as endowments, preferences and production possibilities' (Cass and Shell, 1983).
4. The subject matters of this section have been collected from various issues of different national level newspapers, specially Calcutta Commercial Gazette and Investors Guide.
5. During the slump that followed the post-war boom, many companies came to grief, leading to huge waste of public money. This aroused a public clamour for an enquiry into the organisation and working of the Bombay Stock Exchange. Accordingly, the Atlay Enquiry Committee was appointed by the Government of Bombay on 14 September, 1923. The Committee submitted its reports in early 1924 disclosing much laxity in the administration of the Bombay Stock Exchange. But the recommendation of the Committee did not materialize and as a result the state of the market in no way was improved.
6. After First World War boom, speculative fires were again building on the Bombay Stock Exchange and led to another kind of collapse in 1925 similar to what we saw earlier. After that the securities contract control Act of 1925 was enacted but failed to improve the market position and crisis occurred rather frequently—in 1928, 1930, 1935 & 1936 resulting huge losses to the investing public. This again led to public criticism and demanded for enquiry into the organisation and working of the Bombay Stock Exchange. Accordingly, the Morrison Committee was appointed in November 1936 which submitted its reports in March 1937 recommending different steps to curb the unhealthy speculation.
7. Intrinsic worth is synonymous to 'fair' or 'fundamental' value.
8. One of the strongest investor tendencies documented in both experimental and survey evidence is the tendency to extrapolate or to chase the trend. Trend chasers buy stocks after they rise and sell stocks after they fall.
9. Throughout the decade 80s, the government initiated a number of economic measures which include decontrol and delicensing of industries, relaxation of Monopolistic and Restrictive Trade Practices and Foreign Exchange Regulation Acts, import liberalisation of capital goods and export promotion of consumer products, restructuring of fiscal policy, disinvestment of public sector and boost up of private sector, abolition of Controller of Capital Issues etc.
10. The extent of growth can easily be measured by the fact that as against an annual average amount of just Rs. 90 crores raised from the new issue market in the seventees, a delightful figure of Rs. 6,000 crores has been raised during 1989–90. There was a virtual explosion in the average daily turnover which on the Bombay Stock Exchange alone has shot up from about Rs. 10 crores in 1979–80 to about Rs. 125 crores in 1989–90. Market capitalisation witnessed a massive increase from Rs. 3500 crores to about Rs. 60,000 crores between 1981 and 1990, which was well ahead of other developing countries except Brazil. In terms of number of listed companies which increased from 2265 in 1980 to 6000 in 1990, India was next only to the USA. The number of shareholders

has also risen sharply from about a million to about 15 million during the period, catapulting this nation to the position of being the third largest shareholding population nation in the world, next only to the USA and Japan. To accommodate the first growing needs of investing public, number of stock exchanges also increased from 8 in 1978 to as many as 18 in 1990 while that of active stock brokers shot up from 1250 to 3000 during the period.

11. When the share price indices increased, the Cassandras were prophesying: "The boom seems to be unreal and somewhat illogical", "It is a run away boom" etc. The policy makers warned the investors about speculation: "The market is overheated and if it crashes it could hurt the investors", hence, "Investors should exercise caution when entering the market". These are the few comments that appeared in the different financial weeklies, namely Business India (March 16–19, 1992) etc.
12. The professionals of Financial Institutions opined: "Industry turns the corner and the share market matures", "The present boom in the market is the beginning of an economic miracle in the country", etc. (Widely quoted remarks in different financial weeklies at that time).
13. The government directed a large number of agencies, namely, the Reserve Bank of India (RBI), the Central Bureau of investigation (CBI), the Income Tax Department, the Directorate of Enforcement, the Joint Parliamentary Committee (JPC) etc., to investigate various aspects of the scam.

REFERENCES

Ball, Ray and Phillip Brown. "An Empirical Evaluation of Accounting Income Numbers", *Journal of Accounting Research*, 6 (Autumn, 1968), pp. 159–78.

Bachelier, Louis. "*Theorie de la Speculation*" (Paris, Gauthier Villars, 1900), and reprinted in English in Cootner (ed.), 1964.

Baumol, William J. "Speculation, Profitability and Stability", *Review of Economics and Statistics*, 39 (August 1957), pp. 263–71.

Beckers, S. "Standard Deviations Implied in Option Prices as Predicators of Future Stock Price Variability", *Journal of Banking and Finance*, 5 (September 1981), pp. 363–82.

Beckers, S. "Variances of Security Prices Returns Based on High, Low and Closing Prices", *Journal of Business*, Vol, 56, No. 1 (1983), pp. 97–112.

Black, Fisher. "Noise", Journal of Finance, Vol. XLI, No. 3 (July 1986), pp. 529–543.

Blanchard, O. and M. Watson. "Bubbles, Rational Expectations and Financial Markets" in Crises in the Economic and Financial Structure, ed. by P. Watchtel. Lexington Mass: Lexington Books (1982).

Boldt, Bob L. and Hall L. Arbit. "Efficient Markets and the Professional Investor", *Financial Analysts Journal* (July–August 1984), pp. 22–33.

Case, Karl, E. and Robert, J. Shiller. "The Behaviour of Home Buyers in Boom and Post-Boom Markets", *New England Economic Review* (November/December 1988), pp. 29–45.

Cass, D. and Shell, K. "Do Sunspots Matter?", *Journal of Political Economy,* (1983), Vol. 91, No. 2.

Cootner, Paul (ed.). *The Random Character of Stock Market Prices.* Cambridge: M.I.T., 1964.

Cox, J.C. and Rubinstein, M. "*Option Markets*", Englewood Cliffs, N.J.: Prentice Hall (1985).

Cootner, P. "Stock Prices: Random vs. Systematic Changes", *Industrial Management Review,* 3 (Spring 1962), pp. 24–45.

Cutler, David, James Poterba and Lawrence Summers. "Speculative Dynamics", *Working Paper,* June 1989.

Delong, J. Broadford, Andrei Shleifer, Lawrence H. Summers, and Robert J. Waldman. "The Size and Incidence of the Losses from Noise Trading", *Journal of Finance,* Vol. XLIV, No. 3 (July 1989), pp. 681–696.

Delong, J. Broadford, Andrei Shleifer, Lawrence H. Summers, and Robert J. Waldman. "Positive Feedback Investment Strategies and Destabilizing Rational Speculation", *Journal of Finance,* Vol. XLV, No. 2 (June 1990a), pp. 379–395.

Delong, J. Broadford, Andrei Shleifer, Lawrence H. Summers, and Robert J. Waldman. "Noise Trader Risk in Financial Markets", *Journal of Political Economy,* Vol. 98, No. 4 (1990b), pp. 703–737.

Delong, J. Broadford, Andrei Shleifer, Lawrence H. Summers, and Robert J. Waldman. "The Survival of Noise Traders in Financial Markets", *Journal of Business,* Vol. 64, No. 1 (1991), pp. 1–19.

Dreman, David N. "Psychology and the Stock Market", *AMACOM,* 135 West 50th Street, New York, N.Y. 10020 (1977).

Eatwell, J., Milgate, M. and Newman, P. "*The New Palgrave: A Dictionary of Economics*", London: MacMillan, (1987) (eds.).

Fama, Eugene F. "The Behavior of Stock Market Prices", *Journal of Business,* 38 (January 1965), pp. 34–105.

Fama, Eugene F. "Efficient Capital market: A Review of Theory and Empirical Work", *Journal of Finance* (May 1970), pp. 383–417.

Fama, Eugene F. and Marshall Blume. "Filter Rules and Stock Market Trading Profits", *Journal of Business,* 39 (Special Supplement, January 1966), pp. 226–41.

Fama, Eugene F., L. Fisher, M. Jensen, and R. Roll. "The Adjustment of Stock Prices to New Information", *International Economic Review* (February 1969), pp. 1–21.

Farrel, Michael J. "Profitable Speculation", *Economica,* 33 (May 1966), pp. 183–193.

Figlewski, S. "Subjective Information and Market Efficiency in a Betting Market", *Journal of Political Economy,* Vol. 87 (1979), pp. 75–88.

Friedman, Milton. "The Case for Flexible Exchange Rates", In Essays in Positive Economics, Chicago: Univ. Chicago Press, 1953.

Gadgil, D.R. *The Industrial Evolution of India,* Oxford University Press, Madras (1929).

Galbraith, John K. *The Great Crash,* (Boston: Houghton Mifflin Co. 1961), p.9.

Garber, Peter M. "Famous First Bubbles", *Journal of Economic Perspectives,* Vol. 4, No. 2 (Spring 1990), pp. 35–54.

Garman, M. and M. Klass. "On the Estimation of Security Price Volatilities from Historical Data", *Journal of Business,* Vol. 3, No. 1 (1980), pp. 67–78.

Goldsmith, Raymond W. *"The Financial Development of India, 1860–1977"*, Oxford University Press, Delhi (1983), p. 91.

Grossman, Sanford J. "On the Efficiency of Competitive Stock Markets Where Traders have Diverse Information", *Journal of Finance*, 31 (May 1976), pp. 573–85.

Grossman, Sanford J. "The Existence of Futures Markets, Noisy Rational Expectations and Informational Externalities", Review of Economic Studies, 44(3), (September 1977), pp. 431–49.

Grossman, Sanford J. "Further Results on Informational Efficiency of Competitive Stock Markets", *Journal of Economic Theory*, 18 (June 1978), pp. 81–101.

Grossman, Sanford J. and Joseph E. Stiglitz. "Information and Competitive Price System", *American Economic Review*, 66 (May 1976), pp. 246–53.

Grossman, Sanford J. and Joseph E. Stiglitz. "On the Impossibility of Informationally Efficient Markets", *American Economic Review*, 70 (June 1980), pp. 393–408.

Gupta, Umrao L. *Working of Stock Exchanges in India*, Thomson Press (India) Limited, New Delhi (1972).

Harris, L. "S & P 500 Cash Stock Price Volatilities", *Journal of Finance*, Vol. XLIV, No. 5, (December 1989), pp. 1155–1175.

Jensen, Michael C. "Some Anomalous Evidence Regarding Market Efficiency", *Journal of Financial Economics*, 6 (June–September 1978), pp. 95–102.

Jones, P. and W. Wilson. "Is Stock Price Volatility Increasing?" *Financial Analysts Journal* (November–December, (1989), pp. 20–26.

Keynes, J.M. *The General Theory of Employment, Interest and Money*, London: MacMillan (1976), p. 157.

Kleidon, Allan, W. "Variance Bounds Tests and Stock Price Valuation Models", *Journal of Political Economy*, 94 (October 1986), pp. 953–1001.

Kritzman, Mark. "What Practitioners Need to Know. . . . About Estimating Volatility", *Financial Analysts Journal* (July–August 1991), pp. 22–25.

Krugman, Paul. "Is the Strong Dollar Sustainable?", The U.S. Dollar—Recent Developments, Outlook and Policy Options, Federal Reserve Bank of Kansas City, 1985.

Kunitomo, Naoto. "Improving the Parkinson Method of Estimating Security Price Volatilities", *Journal of Business*, Vol. 65, No. 2 (1992), pp. 295–302.

Kyle, A.S. "Continuous Auctions and Insider Trading", *Econometrica*, 47 (1985), pp. 1315–1336.

Le Roy, Stephen F. and Porter, Richard D. "The Present Value Relation: Test Based on Implied Variance Bounds", *Econometrica*, 49 (May 1981), pp. 555–74.

Lintner, John. "Security Prices, Risk, and Maximum Gains from Diversification", *Journal of Finance*, 20 (December 1965), pp. 587–615.

Mandelbrot, B. "Forecasts of Future Prices, Unbiased Markets, and Martingale Models", *Journal of Business* (January 1986), pp. 242–255.

Mandelbrot, B. "The Variation of Certain Speculative Prices" *Journal of Business*, 36 (October 1963), pp. 394–419.

Marsh, Terry A. and Robert C. Merton. "Dividend Variability and Variance Bound Tests for the Rationality of Stock Market Prices", Working paper 1584–84 (Massachusetts Institute of Technology, Alfred P. Sloan School of Management, 1984).

Messe, Richard. "Testing for Bubbles in Exchange Markets: A Case of Sparking Rates?", *Journal of Political Economy*, 94 (April 1986), pp. 345–73.

Niederhoffer, V. and M.F.M. Osborne. "Market Making and Reversal on the Stock Exchange", *Journal of the American Statistical Association*, 61 (December 1966), pp. 897–916.

Osborne, M.F.M. "Periodic Structure in the Brownian Motion of Stock Prices", *Operations Research*, 10 (May–June 1962), pp. 345–79.

Parkinson, Michael. "The Extreme Value Method for Estimating the Variance of the Rate of Return", *Journal of Business*, Vol. 53, No. 1 (1980), pp. 61–65.

Ross, Stephen A. "Information and Volatility: The No-Arbitrage Martingale Approach to Timing and Resolution Irrelevancy", *Journal of Finance*, Vol. XLIV, No. 1 (March 1989), pp. 1–17.

Samuelson, Paul A. "Proof that Properly Anticipated Prices Fluctuate Randomly", *Industrial Management Review* (Spring 1965), pp. 41–49.

Samuelson, Paul A. "Stochastic Speculative Price", *Proc. Nat. Acad. Sci.*, 68 (February 1971), pp. 335–37.

Schwert, G.M. "Why Does Stock Market Volatility Change Over Time?", *Journal of Finance*, Vol. XLIV, No. 5, (December 1989), pp. 1115–1153.

Schwert, G.M. "Stock Market Volatility", *Financial Analysts Journal* (May–June 1990), pp. 23–24.

Sharpe, William F. "Capital Asset Prices: A Theory of Market Equilibrium and Conditions of Risk", *Journal of Finance*, 19 (September 1964), pp. 425–453.

Shiller, Rober J. "The Use of Volatility Measures in Assessing Market Efficiency", *Journal of Finance*, 36 (May 1981a), pp. 291–304.

Shiller, Robert J. "Do Stock Prices Move too Much to be Justified by Subsequent Changes in Dividends?", *American Economic Review*, 71 (June 1981b), pp. 421–36.

Shiller, Robert J. "Stock Prices and Social Dynamics", *Brooking Papers on Economic Activity*, 2 (1984), pp. 457–498.

Shiller, Robert J. "Fashions, Fads and Bubbles in Financial Markets", paper prepared for Conference on Takeover and Contests for Corporate Control (February 1986).

Shiller, Robert J. "Investor Behavior in the October 1987 Stock Market Crash: Survey Evidence", *NBER Working Paper 2446* (November 1987).

Shiller, Robert J. "Speculative Prices and Popular Models", *Journal of Economic Perspectives*, Vol. 4, No. 2 (Spring 1990), pp. 55–65.

Shiller, Robert J., Fumiko Kon-ya, and Yoshiro Tsutsui. "Investor Behavior in the October 1987 Stock Market Crash: The Case of Japan", *Journal of the Japanese and International Economics*, 5 (1991), pp. 1–13.

Shiller, Robert J. and John Pound. "Survey Evidence on Diffusion of Interest and Information Among Investors", *Journal of Economic Behavior and Organisation*, 12 (1989), pp. 47–66.

Shleifer, Andrei and Lawrence H. Summers. "The Noise Trader Approach of Finance", *Journal of Economic Perspectives*, Vol. 4, No. 2 (Spring 1990), pp. 19–33.

Smith, Vernon L., Gerry L. Suchanek, and Arlington W. Williams, "Bubbles, Crashes and Endogenous Expectations in Experimental Spot Asset Markets", *Econometrica*, Vol. 56, No. 5 (September 1988), pp. 1119–1151.

Stiglitz, Joseph E. "Symposium on Bubbles", *Journal of Economic Perspectives*, Vol. 4, No. 2 (Spring 1990), pp. 13–18.

Summers, Lawrence H. "Does the Stock Market Rationally Reflect Fundamental Values?", *Journal of Finance*, Vol. XLI, No. 3, (July 1986), pp. 591–601.

Telser, Lester G. "A Theory of Speculative Relating Profitability and Stability", *Review of Economics and Statistics*, 41 (August 1953), pp. 295–301.

Tirole, Jean. "On the Possibility of Speculation Under Rational Expectations", *Econometrica*, Vol. 50 (September 1986), pp. 1163–81.

Van Horne, J. "Of Financial, Innovations and Excess", *Journal of Finance*, Vol. 49, No 3, (July 1985), pp. 621–31

West, Kenneth D. "Bubbles, Fads and Stock Price Volatility Tests: A Partial Evaluation", *Journal of Finance*, Vol. XLIII No. 3 (July 1988), pp. 639–656.

Zeckhauser, R., J. Patel, and D. Hendricks. "Nonrational Actors and Financial Market Behavior", *Theory and Decision*, 31 (1991), pp. 257–287.

CHAPTER II

SOME METHODOLOGICAL ISSUES

The main thrust of the present study is to measure current state of market volatility in historical perspective and provide a plausible explanation of this price movement. To investigate these different issues, separate methodologies have been adopted in the present work, mention about which has been made independently in the following two sections.

Section I: Measurement of Stock Price Volatility

Any such study, at the outset, requires to develop a clear concept of "what volatility is?", "how to measure it?", "which data sources to be used?", and "what span of time to be considered?". In a sense, this section deals with different methodological issues relevant to the measurement of share price fluctuation.

Volatility Defined

Volatility means changeability or randomness of asset prices. Theoretically a change in the volatility of either future cash flows or discount rates causes a change in the volatility of share prices. "Fads" or "Bubbles" introduce additional sources of volatility (Schwert, 1989).

From the finance literature, it appears that the operating definition of volatility is the relative dispersion of changes in stock prices relative to some average for a period (Jones and Wilson, 1989). Hence it is usually measured by the standard deviation or variance of stock prices or the rates of return.

Perception of both public and press about stock market volatility, in fact, is largely based on point changes. Finance academicians, however, widely agree that volatility should be measured in terms of percentage change in prices or rates of return, thus discard the use of absolute 'amount' of changes in asset prices. Point changes usually exceed percentage changes because the index levels from where the prices move are often greater than 100 (Jones and Wilson, 1989). Thus the point changes mostly favoured by press, overestimate and create a false impression regarding magnitude of volatility among investors. For obvious reason, present study also relies on percentage changes in prices, or rates of return not on point changes of prices, the approach that is rightly followed by finance economists.

The Measurement

This section aims to examine the problem of estimating stock price volatility parameters from the most available forms of public data. We shall consider below only those volatility estimators that rely on data which are truly universal in their accessibility to investors, namely, the historical opening, closing, high and low prices appearing in the financial pages of different dailies. After evaluating all the parameters, we shall use the volatility estimate, which is most suitable for the nature of data readily available in our country.

In the literature of financial economics, there is the mention of a number of volatility estimators to measure share price fluctuation. All the measures (see Appendix B) may, however, be conveniently clubbed into two broad groups: Close-to-Close standard deviation method and High-Low estimator. Two widely used models representing these groups are discussed below.

1. Close-to-close Standard Deviation Method

The most commonly used measure of stock return volatility is standard deviation based on close-to-close price data (Jones and Wilson, 1989; Schwert, 1990; Cho and Fress, 1988).

Let $(P_1, P_2, ..., P_{n+1})$ be a set of share prices quoted at the close of each trading day. Then the standard deviation of the rate of return (r) on share price, is traditionally estimated as follows: Letting $r_t = I_n (P_t/P_{t-1})$, $t = 1,2,....,n$ = rate of return over the daily closing prices, then

$$\sigma = \left[\frac{1}{n}\sum_{t=1}^{n}(r_t - \bar{r})^2\right]^{1/2}$$

2. High-low Estimator

Market volatility can also be examined by using alternative estimators of volatility, in addition to the standard close-to-close daily price changes. As it is alleged that much of the recent volatility has been in intraday price movements rather than in day-to-day price changes (Edwards, 1988), intuition would tell us that high/low prices contain more information regarding volatility than do close-to-close prices. This intuition is correct. Parkinson (1980) had shown that simply using the daily high (H_t) and low (L_t) prices, the variance estimator $\hat{\sigma}_2^2 = [I_n (H_t) - I_n(L_t)]^{2/4} I_n^2$, had an efficiency of 5.2. It implies about 80% less data (and thus, an 80% smaller time interval) is needed for the extreme value method than for the traditional method (Parkinson, 1980). Thus the use of these extreme values (the high and low prices) provides a far superior estimate to the traditional close-to-close variance.

The principal advantage of the traditional close-to-close standard deviation is its simplicity of use. Closing prices are measured in a consistent fashion from period to period, and there is little question about the time interval being spanned by the estimator (Garman and Klass, 1980). The main disadvantage is, it ignores other readily available information that may be conveniently used to measure fluctuation more efficiently.

The high-low estimator, on the other hand, measures the intraday price movements and thereby reflects much more information. Hence this model may be considered as more efficient than and far superior to the traditional method. It is also very easy to apply in practice provided daily high and low prices are available. The following limitations may, however, blemish otherwise theoretically sound high-low estimator.

First, if the stock does not trade sufficiently there would be no significant difference between high and low prices. Secondly, one may expect bad data points show up more easily in the high and low price quotations. Finally, high and low prices may reflect trades by disadvantaged buyers or sellers and could therefore be less reliable indicators of the true value of the underlying security. Though in general the daily range should give us a better indication of the variability of the price, the aforementioned weaknesses could annihilate this advantage (Backers, 1983).

Whatever might be the strength and weakness of the two estimators, ultimate selection of a particular technique to be used truly depends on the availability of data. The relevant data on intraday high and low share price indices are not available. Hence in the present study close-to-close standard deviation method has been used which is mostly suitable for the data readily available in our country over decades. More details about the method to be used are discussed below. However, for an illustrative purpose, comparative volatility measurement for the year 1990, using two alternative methods is displayed in Figure 2.1.

Two estimates have been measured from the daily high-low and closing prices of top 20 companies by turnover (see Appendix C). The figure suggests that intraday price range estimator is a better measure having lower variance than that of other (Beckers, 1983).

Estimate Used to Measure Volatility

Contemporary finance theories, i.e., the market models are stated in terms of returns rather than prices. The widely accepted concept of rates of return is, of course, the logarithmic difference of prices of two successive periods.[1] This concept is also followed in the present study.

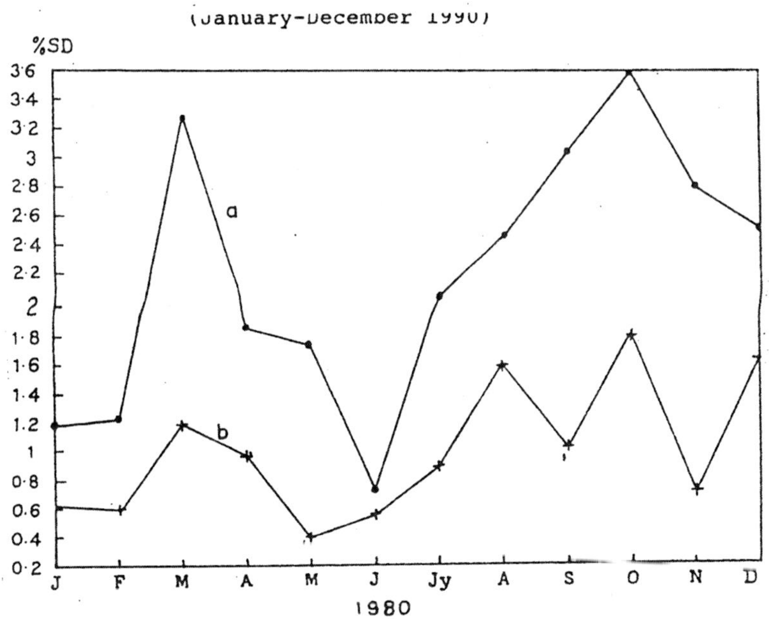

Fig. 2.1. Alternative Estimators of Volatility, Average Daily Share Price of Top 20 Companies by Turnover (January–December 1990)

a. Day-to-day price changes measured by standard deviation of $r_t = I_n(P_{t+1}/P_t)$

b. Intraday price movements measured by standard deviation of In (H/L). This intraday 'price range' estimator is closely related to Parkinson's high-low estimator and provides a more intuitive measure of volatility.

Symbolically, the rate of return (r) is stated as follows:

$$r_t = I_n\ (P_t/P_{t-1}), \qquad t = 1,2,\ldots, n$$

where r_t is the rate of return for the period t, I_n is natural logarithm, and P_{t-1} and P_t are the closing prices for two successive periods (t–1) and t.

This logarithmic transformation expressed in percentage term after multiplying it by 100, represents the continuously compounded (percent) rate of return which, for small changes, is approximately equal to the proportionate price change over the day.[2] It also serves to achieve level stationarity-fluctuations around a constant mean-making the series more amenable to analysis.[3]

As has been mentioned earlier we measure volatility by the standard deviation of rates of return (r), which is a simple but widely used method also most suitable for the nature of data available in our country.

The standard deviation of return (r) from a sample of n observations is the square root of the average squared deviation of returns from the average in the sample. Thus,

$$\sigma = \left[\frac{1}{n}\sum_{t=1}^{n}(r_t - \bar{r})^2\right]^{1/2}$$

where $r_t = I_n(P_t/P_{t-1})$

The logarithmic standard deviation is expressed in percentage term after multiplying it by 100. Depending on the course of the study, standard deviations have been calculated across different earnings, (about which mention has been made in the appropriate sections).

Data Sources

To measure stock market volatility, one commonly used series of data is the index number of share prices (Jones and Wilson, 1989; Harris, 1989; Schwert, 1989, 1990). Hence, the data used in the study are based on different share price indices reported by financial papers.

The sample data consist of mainly two sets. The first set comprises of the "Capital Stock and Share Index", compiled and published by the Capital on monthly basis for a period January 1935 to December 1960. The second one is the series of index number of share prices, namely, "The Economic Times Index Numbers of Ordinary Share Prices", compiled and published by The Economic Times on daily basis for a period 1961 to 1992. The data for the indices have been collected from the various issues of the Capital and the Economic Times for the respective period.

Though share price index is the most commonly used series in any such study, it suffers from some limitations to be reckoned before using it. First, an index may give a completely false impression for the extent of price fluctuations

(Kempt and Reid, 1971). This is because the process of averaging the price changes of different shares may wash out the individualistic portions of the price changes, leaving only the movement that is common to all shares. Secondly, Kendall (1953) has suggested, "Aggregative index numbers behave more systematically than their components. This might be due to the reduction of the random elements by averaging and the consequent emergence of systematic constituents; but it could equally well be due to change."

In spite of these limitations we have no alternative of the index number, specially for the measurement of aggregate share price movement. Hence we have used it as the means to have an end. One should, therefore, keep the above limitations in mind, while interpreting empirical results of our study.

Period Covered

Studies of similar nature in developed countries often consider a longer period of over 100 years in measuring volatility (Jones and Wilson, 1989; Harris, 1989; Schwert, 1989; 1990). But the present study of volatility measurement is confined to a period of only 58 years spanning over 1935–92. Selection of the specific period is primarily guided by some practical considerations, the most important of which is the availability of share price index. To the best of our knowledge, no reliable share price index was readily available before 1935. The Capital started publishing price series on monthly basis since 1935, while the Economic Times daily share price index is available only from 1961. Since none of the price indices was solely available for the entire period, the above two series have been considered successively (1935–'60 and 1961–'62) to cover a relatively long period of time of nearly 6 decades. The period witnessed many big and small events directly or indirectly related with stock market activities.

Simply to measure volatility for a longer period, the validity of using two indices comprising of different portfolios may be questioned. At least there are two points to defend the approach of using two indices in our study.

1. No index maintain the same portfolio for a longer period of time. The portfolio is often reshuffled replacing active by inactive shares. Hence even the use of a single index gives no guarantee that the volatility estimate would be based on same set of shares for the entire period.
2. There is no evidence of significant variation in volatility estimates even when several alternative indices comprising of different portfolios have been used simultaneously to measure it (Schwert, 1989).

In view of the above facts, two indices that represent the most highly traded securities of the respective time period may be conveniently used to cover a relatively longer period.

Section II: Volatility and Market Efficiency

Since in an efficient market, price changes at any time represent the efficient discounting of new information, movement of share prices should be reconciled with the variation in the expectation of future dividends. In this section we discuss the methodology to investigate whether stock price movement in our market can be attributed to subsequent changes in dividends. In the present study we have applied the simple efficient market model and variance inequality tests developed by Robert J. Shiller (1981) to examine the above research question.[4]

The Efficient Market Model

According to the simple efficient market model, the real price P_t of a share at the beginning of the time period t is given by

$$P_t = \sum_{k=0}^{\alpha} y^{k+1} E_t D_{t+k} \qquad 0<y<1 \quad \ldots \quad (1)$$

where D_t is the real dividend paid at (let us say, the end of) time t, E_t denotes mathematical expectation conditional on information available at time t, and y is the constant real discount factor = 1/(1+r), where r is defined to be the constant real interest rate.

The model (1) can be restated in terms of series as a proportion of the long-run growth factor: $p_t = P_t . \lambda^{T-t}$, $d_t = D_t \lambda^{T-t-1}$ where the growth factor is $\lambda^{T-t} = (1+g)^{T-t}$, g is the rate of growth, and T is the base year. The growth factor λ^{T-t} has the effect of eliminating heteroscedasticity due to the gradually increasing size of the market. Multiplying (1) by λ^{T-t} and substituting we find

$$P_t = \sum_{k=0}^{\alpha} (\lambda y)^{k+1} E_t d_{t+k}$$

$$= \sum_{k=0}^{\alpha} \bar{y}^{k+1} E_t d_{t+k} \qquad \ldots \quad (2)$$

The growth rate g must be less than the discount rate r if (1) is to give a finite price, and hence $\bar{y} \equiv \lambda y < 1$, and defining $\bar{r}$ by $\bar{y} \equiv 1/(1+\bar{r})$, the discount rate appropriate for the p_t and d_t series is $\bar{r} > 0$. The discount rate $\bar{r} = E(d)/E(p)$.[5]

The above model may be written in terms of the *ex post* rational price series p_t^* as follows

$$p_t = E_t(P_t^*) \qquad \ldots \quad (3)$$

where
$$p_t^* = \sum_{k=0}^{\alpha} \bar{y}^{k+1} d_{t+k} = \bar{y}(p_{t+1}^* + d_t)$$

Since the summation extends to infinity, we never observe p_t^* without some error. However, with a long enough dividend series we may observe an approximate p_t^*. If we select an arbitrary value for the terminal value of p_t^* then we may determine p_t^* recursively by $p_t^* = \bar{y}(p_{t+1}^* + d_t)$ working backward from the terminal date. If we choose a different terminal condition, the result would be to add or subtract an exponential trend from the p*. As we move back from the terminal date, the importance of the terminal value chosen, however, declines (see Shiller, 1981).

In equation (3), p_t is the mathematical expectation conditional on all information available at time t of p_t^*. In other words, p_t is the optimal forecast of p_t^*. We can define the forecast error as $u_t = p_t^* - p_t$. It can be shown from the theory of conditional expectations that u_t must be uncorrelated with p_t. If u_t is correlated to p_t, then the forecast can be improved.

Since the variance of the sum of two uncorrelated variables is the sum of their variances, we can write

$$\text{var }(p^*) = \text{var }(u) + \text{var }(p)$$

$$\text{or, var }(p) \leq \text{var }(p^*) \quad (\text{since var }(u) \geq 0)$$

$$\text{or, } \sigma\ (p) \leq \sigma\ (p^*) \qquad \ldots \quad (4)$$

The above inequality puts a limit on the standard deviation of p_t in terms of the standard deviation of p_t^*. The efficient market model may be restated in innovation form which allows better understanding of the limits on stock price volatility imposed by the model.

For this purpose, it is convenient to adopt notation for the innovation in a variable. Let us define the innovation operator $\delta_t \equiv E_t - E_{t-1}$ where E_t is the conditional expectations operator. Then for any variable x_t the term $\delta_t\, x_{t+k} = E_t x_{t+k} - E_{t-1} x_{t+k}$ which is the change in the conditional expectation of x_{t+k} that is made in response to new information arriving between t-1 and t. Since conditional expectations operators satisfy $E_j E_k = E_{min}$ (j,k) it follows that $E_{t-m}\, \delta_t\, x_{t+k} = E_{t-m}(E_t\, x_{t+k} - E_{t-1} x_{t+k}) = E_{t-m} x_{t+k} - E_{t-m}\, x_{t+k} = 0$, $m \geq 0$. This means that $\delta_t x_{t+k}$ must be uncorrelated for all k with all information known at time t–1 and must, since lagged innovations are information at time t, be uncorrelated with $\delta_{t'}\, x_{t+j}$, t'<t, all j, i.e., innovations in variables are serially uncorrelated.

The model implies that the innovation in price $\delta_t p_t$ is observable. Since (2) can be written $p_t = \bar{y}(d_t + E_t p_{t+1})$, we know, solving, that $E_t p_{t+1} = p_t / \bar{y} - d_t$. Hence

$$\delta_t p_t \equiv E_t p_t - E_{t-1} p_t = p_t + d_{t-1} - p_{t-1}/\bar{y} = \Delta p_t + d_{t-1} - \bar{r} p_{t-1}$$

The model also implies that the innovation in price is related to the innovations in dividends by

$$\delta_t p_t = \sum_{k=0}^{\alpha} \bar{y}^{k+1}\, \delta_t d_{t+k} \qquad \ldots \quad (5)$$

This expression is identical to (2) except that δ_t replaces E_t. Unfortunately, while $\delta_t p_t$ is observable in this model, the $\delta_t d_{t+k}$ terms are not directly observable, that is, we do not know when the public gets information about a particular dividend. Thus, in deriving inequalities below, one is obliged to assume the "worst possible" pattern of information accural.

To find a limit on the standard deviation of δ_p for a given standard deviation of d_t, first note that d_t equals its unconditional expectation plus the sum of its innovations:

$$d_t = E(d) + \sum_{k=0}^{\alpha} \delta_{t-k} d_t \qquad \ldots \quad (6)$$

If we regard E(d) as $E_{-\alpha}(d_t)$, then this expression is just a tautology. It tells us, though, that d_t, t=0, 1, 2...are just different linear combinations of the same innovations in dividends that enter into the linear combination in (5) which determine $\delta_t p_t$ t=0, 1, 2...Thus it can be asked how large var (δp) might be for given var(d). Since innovations are serially uncorrelated, we know from (6) that the variance of the sum is the sum of the variances:

$$\mathrm{var}(d) = \sum_{k=0}^{\alpha} \mathrm{var}(\delta d_k) = \sum_{k=0}^{\alpha} \sigma_k^2 \qquad \ldots \quad (7)$$

The assumption of stationarity for d_t implies that

$$\mathrm{var}(\delta_{t-k}\, d_t) \equiv \mathrm{var}(\delta d_k) \equiv \sigma_k^2$$

is independent of t.

In expression (5) we have no information that the variance of the sum is the sum of the variances since all the innovations are time t innovations, which may be correlated. In fact, for given σ_0^2, σ_1^2, ..., the maximum variance of the sum in (5) occurs when the elements in the sum are perfectly positively correlated. This means then that so long as

$$\mathrm{var}(\delta d) \neq 0,\ \delta_t\, d_{t+k} = a_k \delta_t d_t, \text{where } a_k = \sigma_k / \sigma_0$$

Substituting this into (6) implies

$$\hat{d}_t = \sum_{k=0}^{\alpha} a_k\, \varepsilon_{t-k} \qquad \ldots (8)$$

where $d_t \equiv d_t - E(d)$ and $\varepsilon_t \equiv \delta_t\, d_t$. Thus, if var (δ_p) is to be maximised for given $\sigma_0^2, \sigma_1^2, \ldots$, the dividend process must be a moving average process in terms of its own innovations. It can thus be shown, rather than assumed, that if the variance of δ_p is to be maximised, the forecast of d_{t+k} will have the usual ARIMA form as in the forecast popularized by Box and Jenkins (1970).

We can now find the maximum possible variance for δ_p for given variance of d. Since the innovations in (5) are perfectly positively correlated,

$$\mathrm{var}(\delta_p) = \left(\sum_{k=0}^{\alpha} \bar{y}^{k+1}\, \sigma_k\right)^2$$

To maximise this subject to the constraint

$$\mathrm{var}(d) = \sum_{k=0}^{\alpha} \sigma_k^2$$

with respect to $\sigma_0, \sigma_1, \ldots$, one may use the Lagrangean:

$$L = \left(\sum_{k=0}^{\alpha} \bar{y}^{k+1}\, \sigma_k\right)^2 + \upsilon\left(\mathrm{var}(d) - \sum_{k=0}^{\alpha} \sigma_k^2\right) \qquad \ldots (9)$$

where υ is the Lagrangean multiplier. The first-order conditions for σ_j, j = 0, ... α are

$$\frac{\delta L}{\delta \sigma_j} = 2\left(\sum_{k=0}^{\alpha} \bar{y}^{k+1}\, \sigma_k\right)\bar{y}^{j+1} - 2\upsilon\sigma_j = 0 \qquad \ldots (10)$$

which in turn means that σ_j is proportional to $\bar{y}^j$. The second-order conditions for a maximum are satisfied, and the maximum can be viewed as a tangency of an isoquent for var (δp), which is a hyperplane in $\sigma_0, \sigma_1, \sigma_2, \ldots$ space, with the hypersphere represented by the constraint. At the maximum $\sigma_k^2 = (1-\bar{y}^2)\,\mathrm{var(d)}\,\bar{y}^{2k}$ and $\mathrm{var}(\delta_p) = \bar{y}^2 \mathrm{var(d)}/(1-\bar{y}^2)$ and so, converting to standard deviations for ease of interpretation, we have

$$\sigma(\delta_p) \le \sigma(d)/\sqrt{\bar{r}_2} \qquad \ldots (11)$$

where $\bar{r}_2 = (1+\bar{r})^2 - 1$

The maximum occurs, then, when d_t is a first order autoregressive process, $\hat{d}_t = \bar{y}\hat{d}_{t-1} + \varepsilon_t$, and $E_t\hat{d}_{t+1} = \bar{y}^k\hat{d}_t$, where $\hat{d} \equiv d - E(d)$ as before.

Other inequality analogous to (11) can also be derived in the same way. We can put an upper bound to the standard deviation of the change in price (rather than the innovation in price) for given standard deviation in dividend. The only difference induced in the above procedure is that Δp_t is a different linear combination of innovations in dividends.

Using $\Delta p_t = \delta_t\, p_t + \bar{r}p_{t-1} - d_{t-1}$ we find

$$\Delta p_t = \sum_{k=0}^{\alpha} \bar{y}^{k+1}\, \delta_t d_{t+k} + \bar{r}\sum_{j=1}^{\alpha} \delta_{t-j} \sum_{k=0}^{\alpha} \bar{y}^{k+1}\, d_{t+k-1} - \sum_{j=1}^{\alpha} \delta_{t-j} d_{t-1} \qquad \ldots (12)$$

As above, the maximisation of the variance of δ_p for given variance of d requires that the time t innovations in d be perfectly correlated (innovations at different times are necessarily uncorrelated) so that again the dividend process must be forecasted as an ARIMA process. However, the parameters of the ARIMA process for d which maximise the variance of Δp will be different. After maximising the

Lagrangean expression [analogous to (9)] an inequality slightly different from (11), is given by

$$\sigma(\Delta p) \leq \sigma(d) / \sqrt{2\bar{r}} \qquad \ldots (13)$$

The upper bound is attained if the optimal dividend forecast is first-order autoregressive, but with an autoregressive coefficient slightly different from that which induced the upper bound to (11). The upper bound to (13) is attained if $\hat{d}_t = (1-\bar{r})\hat{d}_{t-1} \pm \varepsilon_t$ and $E_t\, d_{t+k} = (1-\bar{r})^k \hat{d}_t$, where, as before, $\hat{d}_t \equiv d_t - E(d)$.

The definitions and terminologies are illustrated in Table 2.1.

As referred earlier, we apply the variance inequalities (4), (11) and (13) to test the stock price volatility of our market, using the data set given below.

Data Set and Time Period

To conduct an empirical study of present nature, the commonly used series of data are the index number of share price and dividend series accruing to the portfolio represented by the shares in the price index. Since no such data package is readily available, we have to construct both the price index and dividend series based on same sample companies. Sample companies were selected on the basis of the following criteria:

(1) accounting year must end on 31st March each year,
(2) companies must pay regular dividend, and
(3) their shares must be regularly traded in the market.

Based on above criteria, 30 shares[6] across different industries were chosen to construct the initial portfolio. However, it was necessary to reshuffle the portfolio time to time mainly to replace active by inactive shares. In the course of reshuffling also, only the companies that satisfy the above criteria were considered. The volatility tests are not affected by time to time reshuffling of portfolio, so long as the volatility of the price and dividend series are not misstated (Shiller, 1981).

Table 2.1. Definition of Principal Symbols

y	= real discount factor for series before detrending; $y = 1/(1+r)$
$\bar{y}$	= real discount factor for detrended series; $\bar{y} \equiv \lambda y$
D_t	= real dividend accruing to stock price index (before detrending)
d_t	= real detrended dividend; $d_t \equiv D_t \cdot \lambda^{T-t-1}$
Δ	= first difference operator $\Delta x_t \equiv x_t - x_{t-1}$
δt	= innovation operator; $\delta_t x_{t+k} \equiv E_t x_{t+k} - E_{t-1} x_{t+k}$; $\delta_x \equiv \delta_t x_t$
E	= unconditional mathematical expectation operator. $E(x)$ is the true (population) mean of x.
E_t	= mathematical expectations operator conditional on information at time t; $E_t x_t \equiv E(x_t / I_t)$ where I_t is the information set known at time t.
λ	= trend factor for price and dividend series; $\lambda \equiv 1 + g$ where g is the long-run growth rate of price and dividends
P_t	= real stock price index (before detrending)
p_t	= real detrended stock price index; $p_t = P_t$. T-t
p_t^*	= ex post rational stock price index (expression 3)
r	= one-period real discount rate for series before detrending
$\bar{r}$	= real discount rate for detrended series; $\bar{r} = (1-\bar{y})/\bar{y}$
$\bar{r}_2$	= two-period real discount rate for detrended series; $$\bar{r}_2 = (1+\bar{r})^2 - 1$$
t	= time (year)
T	= base year for detrending and for wholesale price index

The price series P_t for 1968–1991 is the monthly average price of 30 select shares for March when dividend was declared, divided by the average Wholesale Price Index for the year scaled to 1 in the base year 1991 (Shiller, 1981). The dividend series D_t is the average dividends for the calender year ending March, accruing to the portfolio represented by the shares in the price series, divided by the same Wholesale Price Index of the year scaled to 1 in the base year 1991.

The relevant data used to construct the price and dividend series have been collected from different sources, namely various issues of The Economic Times, Calcutta; The Stock Exchange Official Directory, Bombay; and The Reserve Bank of India Bulletin, Bombay.

The variable p_t for 1968–91 is the P_t times a scale factor λ^{T-t}. The variable d_t for the corresponding period is the real total dividends D_t times λ^{T-t-1}.

The period of the study is confined to only 24 years spanning over 1968–1991. Admittedly, it is a short period for a study of this nature. However, there is no readily available data package required for this type of analysis as mentioned earlier, that restrains us for considering a longer period of time.

NOTES

1. The rate of return is simply the logarithmic difference of closing prices of two successive periods and symbolically measured as $I_n(P_{t+1}/P_t)$, where P_{t+1} and P_t are closing prices on two successive days. The mathematical definition of return, $r=I_n(P_{t+1}/P_t)$, has been established by the reasoning stated below.

   Suppose at period 't' the price of a share is P_t and at period 't+1', the price is P_{t+1}. Now, if return accrues @ r% from period 't' to 't+1', then

   $$P_{t+1}=P_t(1+r).$$

   If return accrues semi-periodically, on compound basis, the terminal value at the end of the semi-period would be,

   $$P_{t+\frac{1}{2}} = P_t(1+r/2)$$

   and at the end of the period 't+1'

   $$P_{t+1}=P_t(1+r/2)^2$$

   The terminal value at the end of the period 't+1', for a share price P_t (at period t) compounding 'm' times a period is,

   $$P_{t+1}=P_t(1+r/m)^m$$

   when $m \to \alpha$

   $$P_{t+1} = P_t \underset{m\to\alpha}{Lt} (1+r/m)^m$$

   $$= P_t e^r \quad [\text{Since}, \underset{m\to\alpha}{Lt}(1+r/m)^m = e^r]$$

   $$\text{or, } e^r = P_{t+1}/P_t$$

   $$\text{or, } r = I_n(P_{t+1}/P_t)$$

2. $r_t = I_n(P_t/P_{t-1})$
   percentage return, i.e.,

   $$x_t = 100r_t = 100\, I_n(P_t/P_{t-1})$$

$$\frac{d(I_n x)}{dx} = \frac{1}{x}$$

or, $d(I_n x) = dx/x$ treating d as the differential operator. If the change in x is small, this relationship can be written as:

change in $I_n x$=relative change in x

$$\text{or, } (I_n x_t - I_n x_{t-1}) = (x_t - x_{t-1})/x_{t-1}$$

3. Log percentage change is a simple concept and has the advantage of symmetry in measuring from a high to a low or a low to a high. For example, share price falls 10 points from 100 to 90. The arithmetic percentage decrease is 10%. To get from the low back to the high, however, would require an asymmetric increase of 11.1 percentage. With log percentage changes, the movement from high to low is 100 I_n (90/100) or minus 10.53 per cent: the movement from the low to the high is 100 I_n (100/90) or plus 10.53 per cent. Thus log percentage change serves stationary movement of ups and downs.
4. In developing the variance inequality tests from Efficient Market Model, we have grossly used the writings of Robert J. Shiller (1981).
5. Taking unconditional expectations of both sides of equation (2) we find,

$$E(p) = \frac{\bar{y}}{1-\bar{y}} E(d)$$

using $\bar{y} = 1/(1+\bar{r})$ and solving we find $\bar{r} = E(d)/E(p)$

6. The list of 30 shares initially used for P_t and D_t series are shown in Appendix D.

REFERENCES

Beckers, S. "Variances of Security Prices Returns Based on High, Low, and Closing Prices", *Journal of Business*, Vol. 56, No. 1 (1983), pp. 97–112.

Box, G.E.P. and G.M. Jenkins. Time Series analysis for Forecasting and Control, San Francisco: Holden-Day 1970.

Cho, D. Chinhyung and Edward W. Frees. "Estimating the Volatility of Discrete Stock Prices", *Journal of Finance*, Vol. XLIII, No. 2 (June 1988), pp. 451–65.

Edwards, Franklin R. "Does Futures Trading Increase Stock Market Volatility?" *Financial Analysts Journal* (January–February 1988), pp. 63–69.

German, M. and M. Klass. "On the Estimation of Security Price Volatilities from Historical Data", *Journal of Business*, Vol. 53, No. 1 (1980), pp. 57–78.

Harris, L. "S & P 500 Cash Stock Price Volatilities", *Journal of Finance*, Vol. XLIV, No. 5 (December 1989), pp. 1155–1175.

Jones, P. and W. Wilson. "Is Stock Price Volatility Increasing?", *Financial Analysts Journal* (November–December 1989), pp. 20–26.

Kemp, A.G. and G.C. Reid. "The Random Walk Hypothesis and the Recent Behaviour of Equity Prices in Britain", *Economica*, Vol. 38 (1971), pp. 28–51.

Kendall, M.G. "The Analysis of Economic Time Series—Part I Prices", *Journal of the Royal Statistical Society*, Series A (General), Vol. 116, pt. 1 (1953), pp. 11–25.

Parkinson, M. "The Extreme Value Method for Estimating the Variance of the Rate of Return", *Journal of Business*, Vol. 53, No. 1 (1980), pp. 61–65.

Schwert, G.W. "Why Does Stock Market Volatility Change Over Time?", *Journal of Finance*, Vol. XLIV, No. 5 (December 1989), pp. 1115–1153.

Schwert, G.W. "Stock Market Volatility", *Financial Analysts Journal* (May–June 1990), pp. 23–34.

Shiller, Robert J. "Do Stock Prices Move Too Much to be Justified by Subsequent Changes in Dividends?", *American Economic Review* (June 1981), pp. 421–436.

CHAPTER III

MEASUREMENT OF STOCK PRICE VOLATILITY

Volatility means changeability or randomness of asset prices. Theoretically the value of corporate equity clearly depends on the fundamental economic factors. If share price changes in response to fundamental economic factors or information and expectation about them, there is no social cost associated with such volatility. 'Fads' or 'Bubbles' often introduce additional sources of volatility. In that case, increased volatility leads to a perception of greater risk which threatens the wealth of investors (Edwards, 1988).

Throughout the unprecedented share market boom of the 80s there was a growing feeling among investors that the market is behaving irrationally and it is extremely volatile. To investigate the merit of above perception this chapter attempts to measure share price fluctuation in quantitative terms for a long period of time, so as to assess objectively whether the current state of volatility is above or below historical level, which is the main theme of the present study. In the process, we however, for the time being shrug the burden of proving whether price movements can be explained by fundamental economic factors-currently a fanciful research topic in the area of finance.

In Section I, market volatility has been measured for a time span of 58 years (1935–92). It is a sufficiently long period of time. The period witnessed several booms and depressions, war and peace, changes in industrial policy on several occasions, along with many other small and big events directly or indirectly related with stock market activities. Hence, any measure based on such a long period of time can be truly called as an average measure of market volatility. Current level of volatility has been compared with the average measure for an understanding whether it exceeds or falls short of the historical level.

Section II has been intended to provide more informative measurement of price volatility using daily share price index, which is available for a shorter period of 1961–92. As policy debate largely relates to the present behaviour of stock market, the study based on daily share price index for a relatively current period, would facilitate to generate more information regarding the nature and extent of recent stock market volatility helpful for decision making.

Section I: Volatility in Retrospect (1935–1992)

Indian stock market has a long history, but as an agent of development, it has only a few glorious occasions in its credit to reckon. Number of committees[1] were appointed to review functioning of stock market that submitted innumerable suggestions to minimise speculative activities thereby fluctuation of share price. Ironically all these efforts, by and large, ultimately failed to control irrational share price movement that is crippling normal functioning of the market for long. This section measures stock price volatility in historical perspective for an understanding of the nature and extent of the problem.

We have measured fluctuation in share prices using standard deviation of monthly returns within each year for the time period (1935–92). For each year, monthly prices have been converted into natural logarithms and the mean return and the standard deviation have been calculated from log differences between months within each year. This logarithmic standard deviation is expressed in percentage terms after multiplying it by 100. Thus each year standard deviation is measured around a different mean. For each year 12 monthly returns have been used to calculate standard deviation, so there is one point per year in the plot in Figure 3.1

In Figure 3.1, % standard deviation is shown along with the vertical axis and the horizontal axis represents the time

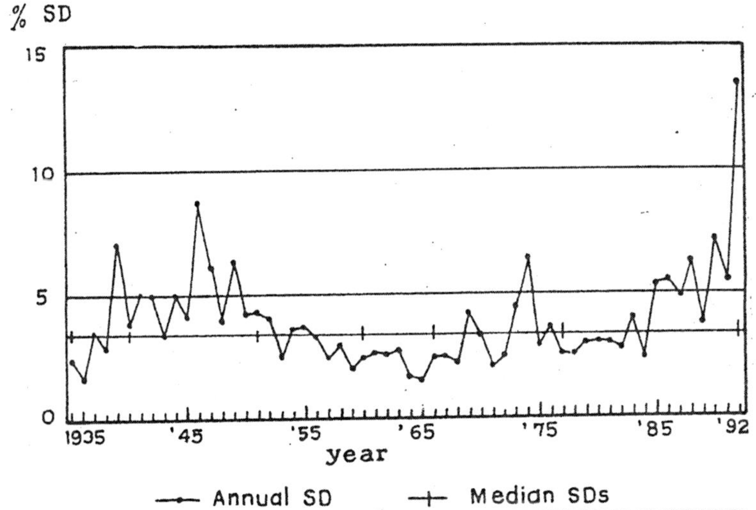

Fig. 3.1. Yearly Standard Deviation of Monthly Return

period. For the complete period, the arithmetic mean of the standard deviation (N = 58) was 3.86106 per cent with a median of 3.41160 per cent. The horizontal line in Figure 3.1 represents the median. For a study of this nature, median is assumed to be the real measure of central tendency as it shows the value of the most central observation. It is unaffected by the presence of extremely large or small observations, thus, the median rather than the mean is shown in the graph by horizontal line (see Jones and Wilson, 1989).

Decadewise analysis of volatility, helpful to evaluate the current state of share price movement relative to one or, more benchmarks, is given below. Means and medians of yearly standard deviation by decade along with variation of earnings in each decade have been arranged in Table 3.1, showing the overall measures at the top. The present measurements do not provide any parametric statistical measures suitable for testing; however, they do allow us to compare the result of recent past with earlier period. Obviously it is a descriptive measure of comparison.

Decadewise analysis along with Figure 3.1 shows violent changes in share prices cluster around the boom of 40s and share mania of 80s that continued up to 1992.

Table 3.1. Decadewise Analysis of Volatility of Monthly Return

Time period	Mean of yearly % SDs	Median of yearly % SDs	Periodic % SD
1935–1992	3.86106	3.41160	4.66685
Subperiod			
1935–1940	3.53081	3.17156	4.14009
1941–1950	5.18306	4.94314	5.72352
1951–1960	3.10824	3.05524	3.43682
1961–1970	2.57516	2.51766	2.82829
1971–1980	2.86692	2.97887	3.69360
1981–1990	4.52840	4.45207	5.07950
1991–1992	9.48943	9.48943	10.29921

The Second World War, war stimulated prosperity, struggle for freedom, independence, partition of country, end of war and beginning of depression are some distinguishing features of decade 40s that make it incomparable to any other period. The war sponsored prosperity eventuated rise in share price almost from the beginning of 1939, and it reached its top at 1946. Following the rules of the market, eclipse followed illumination, the index plunged and downward journey continued upto 1949. Formation and eventual burst of Second World War bubbles during the 40s was the period of extreme volatility of Indian stock market.

Violent fluctuation of the 40s was followed by a tranquil period of more than three decades. Fluctuation was modest, in most of the years, it was even below long range average and there was tired look of share price movement up to 1980.[2] Almost from the beginning of 80s there was an indication of change in the present mood of the market.

Bidding farewell to "control regime", Indian economy was gradually entering into an era of liberalisation from the early 80s. Opening up of the economy, removal of various administrative impediments promised an unprecedented growth and prosperity for the corporate sector. Anticipating good tidings for the private sector, the stock market also started booming. Strong fundamentals eventuated optimism among the investors, ultimately stock market became the new concept of wealth. The time was, therefore, most appropriate for reckless speculation. It inspired few unscrupulous market players most probably at the close of 80s to illegally divert enormous funds from banking sector to finance their operations in the stock market—the scandal that marred the entire economic system—is known as Security Scam.

Flash of money into an already boiling market, accentuated demand and contributed an unbelievable rise in price in 1990–91 and the index hits its top at March 1992. When the scandal was exposed, the government responded harshly, flow of excess money stopped, index plunged from 4500 in March to 2500 in May 1992 and total panic engulfed the stock market. Thus Standard Deviation of return of the decade 80's was very high and in 1991–92 variability of earnings suppressed all previous records. Truly, after independence it was the period of highest volatility that too at a stage of very initial years of liberalisation of Indian economy after prolonged era of control. Experts and policy makers were bewildered specially after the meteoric fall in share price at 1992, doubts were expressed about the capabilities of the market to support the liberalising policy of the government.

Table 3.2. Top 10 Volatile Years

Year	% SDs	Year	% SDs
1992	13.47126	1988	6.40413
1946	8.77574	1949	6.36178
1990	7.23054	1947	6.10532
1939	7.03746	1986	5.56162
1974	6.46553	1991	5.50760

Table of 10 most volatile years shows that 1992 top the list as an exceptionally volatile year, bearing an all time high standard deviation of 13.471%, and it is far ahead of 1946, the second in rank. Among the top 10 years, 4 and 5 belong to 40's and spell of boom of 80's respectively, 1974 is the only outlying year that does not pertain to the major clusters. 1990, 1991 and 1992, three years in a row are included in the list of top ten, the period which may be considered as the most stormy period of Indian stock market.

In the forthcoming section, we propose to take a detailed analysis of the nature and extent of volatility based on daily return for a relatively current period (1961–92) to unveil the reasons and to understand its development implications on our economy. Selection of the period is primarily guided by some practical considerations and the most important among them is the availability of daily share price index necessary for the type of analysis undertaken in the next section. Undenyingly it would have been better if rigorous analysis of following nature could have been carried out for the total period, but nonavailability of daily share price index prevented us from doing so.

Section II: Share Price Fluctuation Revisited (1961–1992)

In the literature of financial economics, there are enough evidences of using monthly share price index to measure volatility and the findings show that in the long run both monthly and daily share price indices reveal identical trend (Schwert, 1989). Obviously, information relating to intramonth movement of share prices gets lost by the use of monthly share price index, hence it is less informative. Minute measurement of volatility based on daily share price index would be helpful for a better understanding of the pattern of volatility of Indian stock market along with the rational and adequacy of the steps taken in the present time to control it.

In this section, on the basis of daily share prices, standard deviations of return for various time period are measured in the same way as described earlier. The only difference is, returns are calculated on daily basis instead of monthly. Thus for each period, on the basis of daily earnings one standard deviation has been calculated.

Table 3.3 exhibits mean and standard deviation of daily return by decade for the period 1961 to 1992. A glance at the table reveals that the decade 80's and the years 1991 and 1992 bear much higher standard deviations as compared to earlier decades.

During the days of violent price fluctuations of the 80's there was a feeble attempt to justify present movement in terms of arrival of information. It was argued, large scale participation of smart money managers, increased awareness of individual investors, use of computer, development of

Table 3.3. Mean and Standard Deviation of Daily Return by Decade, May 1961 to December, 1992

Time period	n	log % Mean	log % SD
1961–1970	2569	0.00654857	0.4808214
1971–1980	2538	0.0248456	0.5563469
1981–1990	2319	0.0667436	1.002394
1991–1992	440	0.159887725	1.55950298
All	7866	0.03877574	0.780449208

communication system, contributed in the capacities of stock market to learn about and to react to information very quickly. Thus the rate at which price changes in response to information has also increased in the recent period. This is an essential feature of efficient market, a cherised belief of some of the financial economists about stock market behaviour.

The scam not only pricked the above academic explanation of capital market behaviour but also made public few flaws of money market, so long ignored by the policy makers. The most important is the prevailing disproportionate rate of interest between artificially segmented "formal" and "informal" market most suitable to arbitrage between them. Rate of interest in the informal money market which finances stock market operation is about 35–40 per cent, in contrast to 18–20 per cent interest[3] in formal money market. Disproportionate rate of interest for "badla" finance by no means can be attributed to the difference in level of risk. Badla enjoys institutional safeguards against nonpayment by the broker, advances are usually made for a short duration (typically a fortnight) and the default rate is exceptionally low. Thus informal money market offers a return that defies any logic.

Under the new economic policy, there was tremendous pressure on public sector units and nationalised banks to perform—in financial terms. This coincided with a growing need for funds in the informal money market to finance stock market operations at very high rates of interest. It inspired government organisations to divert funds in the informal money market to fetch abnormally high rates of return and funds were available in plenty to finance speculative activities of the market. Soon market turned into an arena of gamble and people started behaving in a way as if the concept of "fair value", or "equilibrium price" has little significance in practice, they may simply ignore them without loss.

Monthly Volatility of Daily Return

Till now attention has been given to measure monthly or daily volatility by year or for a further longer period of time by taking only one standard deviation for the entire period. An attempt is made in this section to measure share price fluctuation using standard deviation of daily return within each month. The measurement has been done using same logarithmic percentage terms as in the previous analysis. Each month's standard deviation is measured around a different mean, in the same sense that in the previous analysis the standard deviation for each year was measured around each yearly mean.

Figure 3.2 plots the monthly standard deviations from May, 1961 to December, 1992. The horizontal line again represents the median. For the entire period, the arithmetic mean (N = 380) of this measure is 0.63504 per cent with a median of 0.501805 per cent.

There are in total 380 monthly standard deviation estimates in Figure 3.2, based on daily return of each month. In contrast, Figure 3.1, for the same period, includes only 32 standard deviation estimates, each based on 12 monthly returns per year. Increased volatility for few months is clearly reflected in Figure 3.2, because their intramonth volatilities are not diluted by the monthly volatility of the rest of the year. Showing intramonth price movement, Figure 3.2 thus contains more information in comparison with Figure 3.1.

Table 3.4 displays top 25 volatile months of 32 years. April 1992 stands out as the most volatile month followed by March 1992 and October 1990 as second and third respectively. Interestingly top 3 volatile months of 32 years belong to the most stormy period of Indian stock market that started from 1990. Out of total 25 month, only 2 belong to the calm period of 60's and 70's, 3 and 7 included in first and second half of the 80's respectively. Only 3 years of the 90's top the list with 13 months in its credit, out of which as much as .7 simply

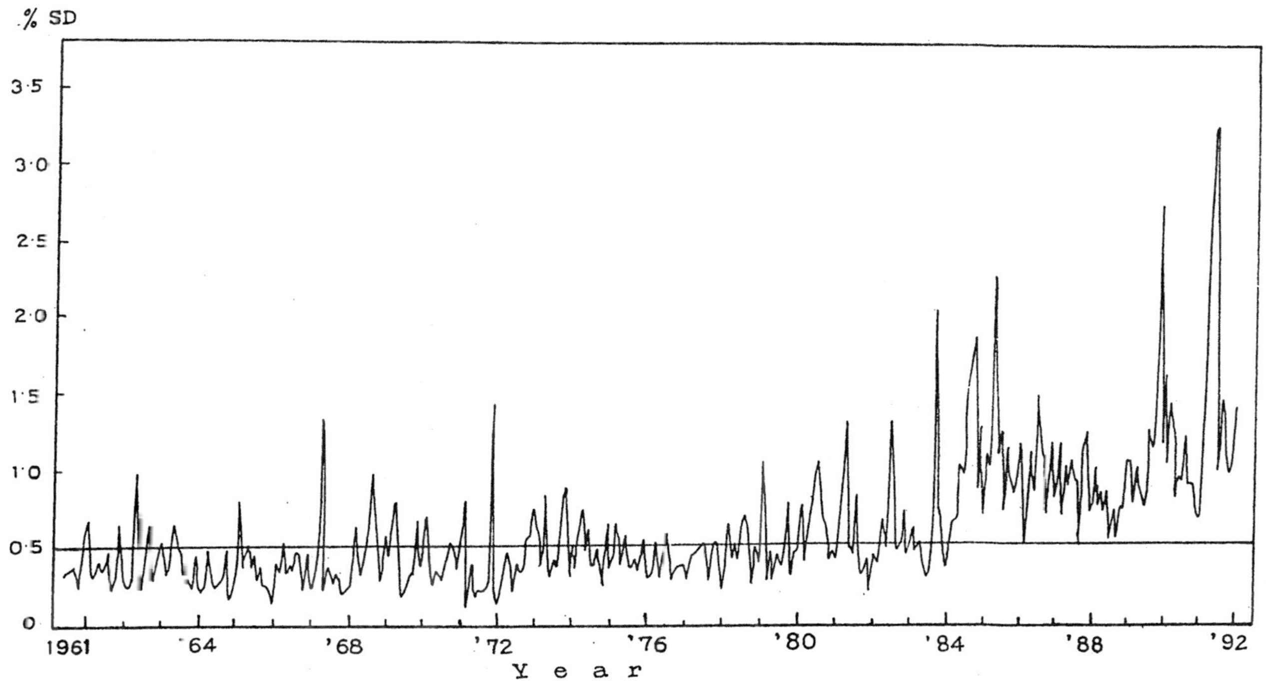

Fig. 3.2. Monthly % SD of Daily Return

Table 3.4. 25 Highest Volatile Months

Rank	Month	Mean Daily Return	% SD
1.	April '92	−0.92589	3.23895
2.	March '92	2.04579	3.17525
3.	October '90	−0.35032	2.7075
4.	March '86	−0.54853	2.24079
5.	May '92	−2.03419	2.07817
6.	August '83	0.06647	2.0036
7.	September '85	−0.49037	1.85105
8.	August '85	−0.28402	1.69488
9.	December '90	−0.38824	1.61524
10.	July '85	0.36605	1.51370
11.	May '87	−0.05418	1.49096
12.	July '92	−0.46776	1.46670
13.	February '91	0.83209	1.44933
14.	October '72	0.09227	1.43535
15.	August '92	0.22214	1.41762
16.	December '92	0.04097	1.39465
17.	February '92	0.69462	1.39242
18.	September '90	0.38762	1.36958
19.	March '68	0.14749	1.35542
20.	June '87	−0.08957	1.33902
21.	May '83	0.52020	1.31902
22.	March '82	−0.21882	1.30377
23.	November '85	0.08632	1.28578
24.	March '91	−0.03659	1.27815
25.	July '90	0.87650	1.27656

pertains to 1992, the most current and volatile year in the history of Indian stock market.

What are the factors that contributed to the gradual rise in volatility? Is it simply fundamental factors or a number of other imperfections responsible for the vociferous movement in share prices?

One of the intuitively appealing explanations combines both fundamental factors and irrational behaviour of investors while interpreting the gradual rise in volatility. Initial boost up of share price, hence fluctuation, apparently owe much to strong fundamentals[4] of the 80's which was supplemented by a number of liberalising policies and procedures of the government. During the rise in prices, "trend chasing" investors seemed to be further encouraged by the optimism extruded by the government, media, leading financial advisers and people like migrating birds entered market in herds. Obviously they joined in clusters, that resulted in a gradual shift in the demand for shares in a basically thin market. When investors were in frenzy, speculators armed with outside money participated in this bandwagon that added fuel to the fire. Price started moving undeviatingly, fluctuations were vehement and it culminated into a record high price in March '92; curiously when Indian economy was in deep crisis.[5] Massive public participation is the classic property of the terminal stage of a bull market and in April 1992 ultimately bubbles burst and price started its downward journey. Thus 1992, the year of meteoric rise and alpine fall of share price stands out as the most volatile year of Indian stock market that alone includes top 7 volatile months of last 32 years.

What was the reaction of the "guardians" of the market in the hey-days of meteoric rise and alpine fall of share price?

During the days of rhythmic fluctuation of the rising index, the government pretended to be an ignoramus about the recent development and was, in fact, complacent with the fund raising capacity of the berserk market. After the scam, the government busy to shrug of its responsibility reacted hastily that instead of restoring normalcy in the market, precipitated abnormal price drop.[6] Total gain in market capitalisation from January 1991 to March 1992 was largely wiped out by the mammoth fall in price in April, May, and July of 1992, leaving a marginal daily return of 0.0159 per cent with a high standard deviation of 1.559 per cent for the period of 1991–92 (see Table 3.4).

Market authorities ritually applied all the mechanisms, namely, change in margin money, volume restrictions, market closure etc. to curb excessive fluctuation but all their efforts were successfully marginalised by omnipotent speculators. In fact, its a perennial problem of Indian stock market. Broker dominated board[7] often makes mockery to all regulations for curbing excessive speculation to promote the selfish interest of members even at the cost of general investors.

Financial institutions, often called as "smart money" managers were neither willing nor capable to combat undesirable influence of noise traders in the market. They instead preferred to fish in the troubled water in their quest to provide short term benefit to its unit holders and suffered a setback alike other naive traders when bubble burst.

Measurement of "Spike" Volatility

Very often it is argued that there is the necessity to differentiate between 'normal' and 'spike' volatility. The latter measure accounts for those unusual days when extreme variations occur.

Movements of share prices in response to arrival of new information are unlikely to be very large and investors need not lose their sleep merely for this type of movements of prices. "Thus investment remains reasonably 'safe' for the individual investor over short periods and hence over a succession of a short period however many, if he can fairly rely on their being no break down in the convention" (Keynes, 1936). Spike volatility interrupts the normal rhythm of share price movement temporarily and increases concern of investors.

Till now we have measured the share price movement by using the standard deviation of daily return. However, the standard deviation estimate is often criticized as a measure of volatility, as it tends to be better at giving a picture of the nature of 'average sized' moves than at revealing much about the propensity of the market to make infrequent, extremely large moves (Greenwald and Stein, 1988). The market's propensity for large moves can be quantified by counting the number of days during a given period in which it moved more than some threshold amount in either direction. In this endeavour, the percentage of days for each year in which logarithmic price change exceed 2 per cent threshold, has been ploted in Figure 3.3. It appears that throughout the period from 1961 to 1980, there has not been significant large swing in prices. Price volatility starts to increase since the beginning of the decade 80's and it got a momentum from 1985, the year in which there were market moves in excess of a 2 per cent threshold on more than 8 per cent of all trading days. But the exceptional price movement occurs during the year 1992, when over 21 per cent of all trading days witnessed swing over ± 2 per cent.

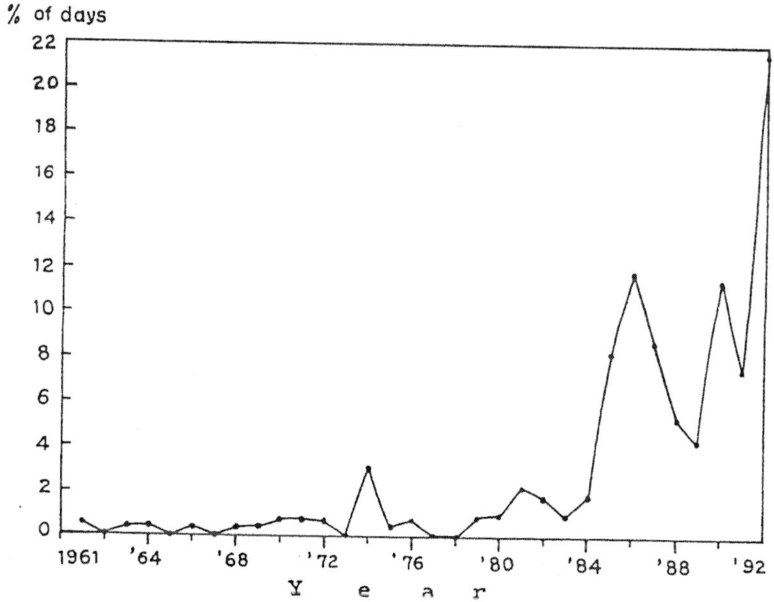

Fig. 3.3. Daily Change > 2 per cent Threshold

We also repeated the same methodology, using threshold of 1 per cent. In that case also, the conclusion is essentially the same; the incidence of extreme price movement virtually started from 1985 and was rampant in 1992 (see Figure 3.4).

In the above analysis, large swings of 1 or 2 per cent were considered as "spike" movements simply on arbitrary basis. Theoretically, 'spikes' are only those 'moves' which lie outside the plus or minus 3 standard deviation limit, as logarithmic price changes are more or less symmetrically distributed like a normal curve. In this endeavour, the logarithmic mean daily price change for the entire period (1961–92), is measured as 0.03877 per cent with a standard deviation of 0.78044 per cent. Tabulation of the spike daily changes thus shows that 135 days out of 7866 trading days in total lie outside a plus or minus limit of 2.34134 per cent (3 × 0.78044 per cent).

Table 3.5 shows number of days per year, when daily percentage change in share prices of either sign was more than 2.34134 per cent along with the total number of days for

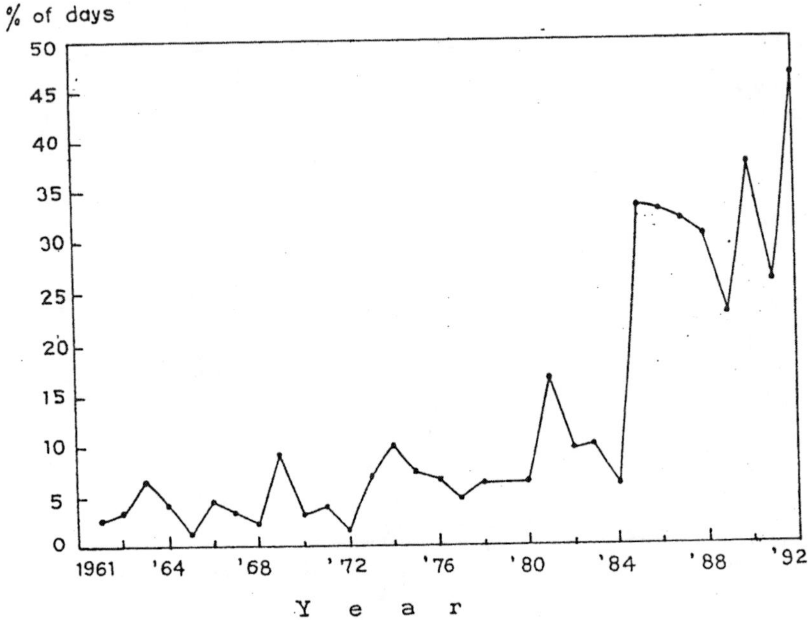

Fig. 3.4. Daily Change > 1 per cent Threshold

the year. As usual 1992 top the list followed by '90 and '86. Interestingly positive and negative changes were equal in 1992 and for other two years positive changes were marginally higher. All these three years were members of top 10 volatile years in the last 58 years. Thus the years with more frequent spikes had higher standard deviations also. Again, even a casual observation of the table gives an impression that the volatility touched a new height from '85. Interestingly positive and negative changes were equal in 1992 and for other two years positive changes were marginally higher. For those, who are interested in exact dates of some of these extreme movements, we have isolated the daily moves of plus or minus above 3 logarithmic percentage changes in Table 3.6 (The cut off point has been raised to 3% so as to make the set manageable). Throughout the period, we have 68 days where daily price changes were more that ± 3%. Among these day, the gainers outnumber the losers by 6 only.

Forces that cause such temporal disequilibrium, according to Keynes, may be described as market fads or animal

Table 3.5. Number of Changes in Daily Prices in Excess of Plus or Minus 2.34134 per cent, May 1961–December 1992

Year	Positive	Negative	Total
1961		1	1
1964		1	1
1966	1		1
1968	1		1
1969		1	1
1970	2		2
1971	1		1
1972	2	1	3
1974	1	2	3
1980	1		1
1981	1	1	2
1982		2	2
1983	1		1
1984	1	1	2
1985	8	4	12
1986	10	7	17
1987	4	2	6
1988	7	1	8
1989	3	1	4
1990	10	9	19
1991	5	2	7
1992	20	20	40
All	79	56	135

sprits.[8] We believe, greater the distance that a price is from its equilibrium level, the greater will be the force pulling the price back towards equilibrium. The "abnormal" price oscillation and 'off setting' process need not be always very precise or predictable but it obviously helps price to move around equilibrium level (Wheeler, 1989). Both Table 3.5 and 3.6 give an impression how this "off setting" process works.

Table 3.6 ranks the days where the ± daily earnings were more than 3 per cent. The table contains a large volume of data from which some interesting observations may be focussed.

The list of dates is dominated by the year 1992 having 10 positive returns and 8 negative returns followed by 1990 and 1986. This is a simple way to show that the mentioned years had higher volatility.

Table 3.6. Daily Price Changes in Excess of Plus or Minus 3 per cent 1961–1992

Rank	Year	Month	Day	+ Change	Rank	Year	Month	Day	–Change
1.	1992	3	2	8.79802	1.	1992	4	28	–6.82122
2.	1992	3	24	7.5036	2.	1984	8	14	–6.71005
3.	1992	3	30	7.01979	3.	1974	7	31	–6.55770
4.	1968	3	4	5.91120	4.	1992	5	11	–6.53827
5.	1990	10	9	5.53879	5.	1985	8	16	–5.94639
6.	1983	5	13	5.41291	6.	1992	4	29	–5.65978
7.	1984	8	13	5.33886	7.	1990	10	15	–5.55863
8.	1991	2	19	5.32284	8.	1990	10	16	–4.84781
9.	1992	4	8	5.24504	9.	1992	5	6	–4.80206
10.	1992	3	3	5.16725	10.	1985	9	4	–4.66046
11.	1986	3	25	4.86522	11.	1990	10	11	–4.53257
12.	1972	10	6	4.50096	12.	1972	10	7	–4.35013
13.	1970	7	25	4.29721	13.	1992	3	10	–4.32226
14.	1980	1	2	3.93028	14.	1963	3	4	–4.27570
15.	1985	9	6	3.89113	15.	1991	3	7	–4.25317
16.	1992	3	31	3.81807	16.	1985	9	30	–4.10308
17.	1986	1	2	3.68633	17.	1986	3	18	–3.97720
18.	1972	1	1	3.66072	18.	1969	7	1	–3.86691
19.	1987	10	5	3.63392	19.	1986	3	3	–3.81488
20.	1991	7	25	3.61768	20.	1982	3	18	–3.74507
21.	1986	6	10	3.50050	21.	1992	7	16	–3.73996
22.	1974	3	1	3.48467	22.	1990	10	12	–3.48420
23.	1988	9	11	3.46159	23.	1981	6	15	–3.46813
24.	1990	8	30	3.32288	24.	1987	5	27	–3.43585
25.	1985	11	20	3.31277	25.	1992	4	6	–3.32542
26.	1992	1	30	3.29003	26.	1987	3	2	–3.31053
27.	1970	2	28	3.25613	27.	1990	11	29	–3.30967
28.	1988	9	30	3.22499	28.	1986	3	7	–3.17869
29.	1988	10	3	3.21655	29.	1991	1	2	–3.10578
30.	1992	2	29	3.16245	30.	1986	8	14	–3.07030
31.	1992	3	25	3.15471	31.	1992	5	27	–3.05972
32.	1988	9	19	3.12686					
33.	1985	7	18	3.11222					
34.	1990	7	30	3.04045					
35.	1992	2	10	3.02639					
36.	1985	5	9	3.00340					
37.	1986	12	9	3.00245					

Relatively stable period of 60's and 70's in total shares only 5 positive and 4 negative changes, whereas 32 and 27 changes belong to the boom of 80's, the most volatile period of Indian stock market. Frequency distribution of the dates of massive changes in share prices during '80 to '92 shows '80 to

'84 have 3 positive and 3 negative changes, '85–'89 include 13 and 9 changes, '90–'92 share 16 and 15 changes respectively. It gives an impression, how the current level of volatility has gradually increased.

Another interesting information that is available from the above table relates to specific dates of ± price movements during the year 1992. Dates of all major positive changes show that it mainly associates with the first quarter of the year, in and around, when the Union budget was placed that provided grandiose concession to capital market. Ironically crazy investors could not even guess the mood of the market that fooled them almost from the start of April.

Interestingly, both the largest positive and negative changes occurred in March and April of 1992, the two most successive volatile months of the highest volatile year. This year being the most turbulent period deserves a detailed analysis for a better understanding of the behaviour of security market.

Out of 7866 trading days, the largest one day price change (+ 8.79802%) occurred on 2nd March 1992, following the presentation of Union budget on 29 February 1992. The next two massive changes (both positive) in share prices took place on 24th and 30th March of 1992. The sequence of top three positive large swings indicates that it has taken about one month for investors to assess the value of new information conveyed by the budget proposal.

The largest negative change in share prices (–6.821%) befell on 28th April 1992, soon after press report about security scam first appeared. The government in its quest to disown responsibility for scam, in quick succession took series of hectic actions[9] that created panic among the investors and brokers. It led to at least 7 steep falls in daily price on different dates, ranging from 7 to 3 per cent approximately in April to December 1992. Only these few major drops account for nearly 35 per cent out of roughly 40 per cent reduction in market value of the stock within nine months.

So far, an attempt was made to unveil the reasons of abnormal price changes only for the most volatile year of 1992. A comprehensive list of information released on the date of large price swings during the most turbulent period of the

Table 3.7. Associated Events Released in the Vicinity of Price Swings in Excess of Plus or Minus 3 Per cent during the Period 1985–1992

Date	Plus or Minus Percentage Change	Release of Information
09.05.85	+3.00340	None
18.07.85	+3.11222	The Government initiates some measures to boost up industrial growth
16.08.85	–5.94639	Financial institutions start disinvesting
04.09.85	–4.66046	Institutional selling continues
06.09.85	+3.89113	Financial Institutions stop disinvestment
30.09.85	–4.10308	Institutional selling starts again
20.11.85	+3.31277	None
02.01.86	+3.68633	None
03.03.86	–3.81488	Presentation of Union Budget (1986–87) on 28.02.86*
07.03.86	–3.17869	None
18.03.86	–3.97720	None
25.03.86	+4.86552	Finance Minister's assurance regarding partial modification of budget proposals
10.06.86	+3.50050	None
14.08.86	–3.07030	None
09.12.86	+3.00245	None
02.03.87	–3.31053	None
27.05.87	–3.43585	None
05.10.87	+3.63392	None
01.09.88	+3.46159	Sustained institutional buying
19.09.88	+3.12686	Sustained institutional buying
30.09.88	+3.22499	Sustained institutional buying
03.10.88	+3.21655	None
25.07.90	+4.29721	Market authority lifts ceiling and withdraws jobbing restriction
30.07.90	+3.04045	None
30.08.90	+3.32288	None
09.10.90	+5.53879	Relaxation of curb trading and lifting ban on forward trading imposed as early as September 1990
11.10.90	–4.53257	Forecast made by leading American investment banker, Merrill Lynch, about

Date	Plus or Minus Percentage Change	Release of Information
		the possibility of a disastrous fall in share prices after Diwali
12.10.90	−3.48420	None
15.10.90	−5.55863	None
16.10.90	−4.84781	None
29.11.90	−3.30967	None
02.01.91	−3.10578	None
19.02.91	+5.32284	The government decides to postpone the presentation of the Union Budget (1991–'92) by a 'few months'
0.7.03.91	−4.25317	The Prime Minister, Mr. Chandra Shekhar, resigns on 06.03.91*
25.07.91	+3.61768	Presentation of the Union Budged (1991–92) on 24.07.91*
30.01.92	+3.29903	RBI concession regarding FERA companies
10.02.92	+3.02639	Stiffer attitude of the Pakistani government towards Amanulla Khan temporarily cools down bitter Indo-Pak relationship
29.02.92	+3.16245	None
02.03.92	+8.79802	Presentation of the Union Budget (1992–93) on 29.02.92*
03.03.92	+5.16725	None
10.03.92	−4.3226	None
24.03.92	+7.5036	Lifting of curbs on trading
25.03.92	+3.15471	None
30.03.92	+7.01979	Relaxation of trading restrictions
31.03.92	+3.81807	New exim policy lifts all major curbs on trade
06.04.92	−3.32542	None
08.04.92	+5.24505	None
28.04.92	−6.82122	Rumour about involvement of big bulls in certain irregularities pertaining to various security deals
29.04.92	−5.65978	The multi-crore securities scam is unveiled
06.05.92	−4.80206	The RBI sets up a committee to inquire into security transactions of banks & financial institutions

(*contd.*)

(*Table 3.7 contd.*)

Date	Plus or Minus Percentage Change	Release of Information
11.05.92	−6.53827	Officials asked to take leave to facilitate the RBI inquiry into the securities scam
27.05.92	−3.05972	The RBI determines to unveil the role of banks and financial institutions in the securities scam
16.07.92	−3.73996	None

Note
Based on information published in various issues of *The Economic Times*, Calcutta, *Business India*, Bombay etc. Information displayed on different dates was released before the closure of the trading sessions of the respective days. However, some information (*) which arrived in the market at a time when there was no scope of incorporating it into the share price (i.e., released after trading sessions, during holidays, etc.) was treated as new information of the next trading day. In the case of some major events (i.e., Union Budgets of 1986–87 & 1992–93, Merrill Lynch's forecast and the securities scam), the market took time to assess fully the value of the new information and there were some chain reactions of subsequent days having no further new information.

Indian stock market, i.e., 1985 to 1992, is given in Table 3.7. This would be helpful for understanding the relative contribution of 'noise'and 'news' of the abnormal price oscillation.

The associated events identified in the table suggest that certain factors such as changes in fundamentals, institutional intervention in the operation of the market, and chain reactions to some major news largely contributed to the abnormal oscillation of share prices at different dates. Curiously enough, for some days, there were no well-defined events implying that the changes could be attributed simply to private information, rumours, occasional 'frenzy' of investors, etc. The reasons for such an irrational movement in share prices and its probable impact on investors' psychology have been extensively researched in the area of financial economics[10] (Shiller, 1981a, b; LeRoy and Porter, 1981; Roll 1988; Schwert, 1989 and 1990). This is an area which deserves a further rigorous study and is beyond the scope of the present study.

Spikeless Fluctuation

Large price changes are likely to reflect the unusual events being occurred in the day-to-day market operation. The presence of these events interrupts the rhythm of the market. With no such disturbing event, market usually operates within a reasonable range of price movement. Thus average volatility is—what price fluctuation would be in the absence of unusual events.

To have an understanding of average volatility we exclude the spike returns above or below $\pm$ 2.3413 per cent and consider only the remainings to measure monthly % SD throughout the period (1961–92) in the same way as followed earlier.

Figure 3.5 plots SD estimates measured on the basis of normal return for the entire period and it shows that the abnormal monthly volatility disappears, while the spike returns are ignored. From 1961–80 the normal level of fluctuation ranged from 0.13744 to 0.80672 per cent. After '80 both lower and upper limits increased, but the latter increased at a higher rate than that of the former. As a result there was an expansion as well as upward shift of the range of price movement.

Conclusion

The study shows that the boom of 40's was a period of excessive volatility in Indian stock market, which was followed by a tranquil period of more than three decades. Since the beginning of 80's price volatility gained momentum once again and reached at the highest peak in 1992. After relative stability of a prolonged era of 30 years, why did market volatility increase in the recent past?

During the days of violent share price fluctuations, there was an attempt to justify present movement in terms of arrival of information. This is an essential feature of efficient market, a cherished belief of some of the financial economists about stock market behaviour (Fama 1970 and Jensen, 1978).

This particular approach of market behaviour though highly acclaimed by academic researchers, was however,

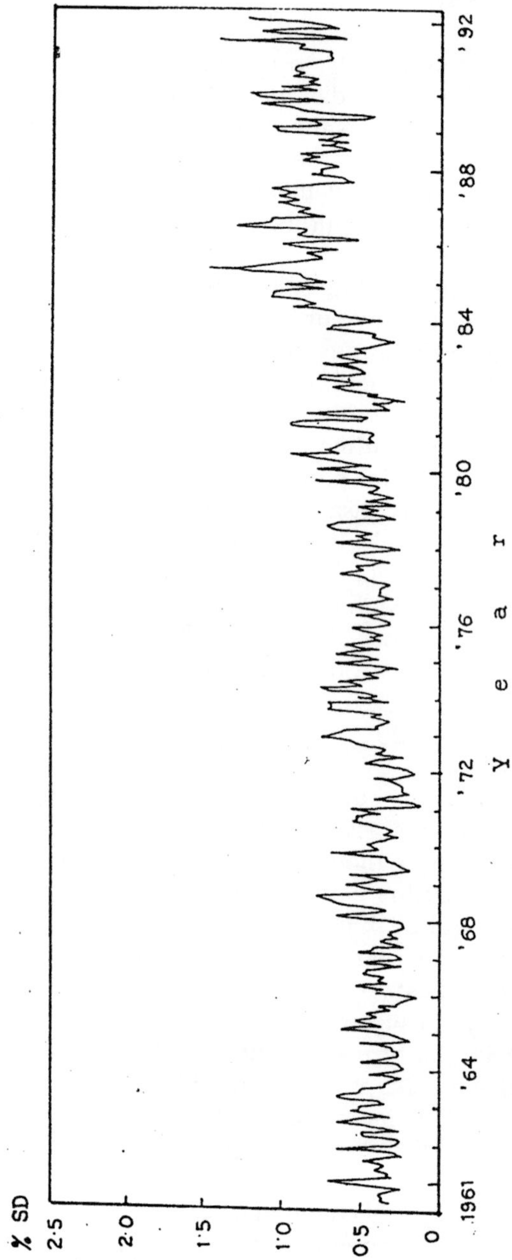

Fig. 3.5. Monthly % Standard Deviation of Normal Return

seriously questioned when news of endless speculation abetted by outside money broke out and crazy investors deserted stock market *en masse*.

There is rally and counter rally on stock price behaviour of current volatile period, hence the debate still remains unresolved. So we propose to investigate vigorously this specific issue in the next chapter.

NOTES

1. It includes the Atlay Committee, the Morison Committee, the Gorwala Committee, the Patel Committee, the Dave Committee, and the Pherwani Committee.
2. It contradicts the finding of Schwert (1989) that volatility tends to increase during depression.
3. It refers to the interest rate of the formal market where banks lend to each other against government securities.
4. Some evidences of encouraging performance of Indian corporate sector (1980–81 to 1989–90):
5. During the period Indian economy all but collapsed on account of Balance of Payment crisis and industry has been in the midst of a deep recession. In any other country, this would immediately be reflected in the stock exchanges, but not so in India.
6. The government promulgated an ordinance which attached the properties of all individuals accused in the scam and also voided all transactions that had at any stage been routed through them after March 31, 1991. The shares which had passed through the hands of accused in the last one year, became "tainted" shares and overnight they became worthless pieces of paper as they could not be delivered in the market.

Year	Industrial growth rate (%)	Equity Dividend as a percentage of paid up equity capital
1980–81	4.0	12.7
1981–82	8.6	13.1
1982–83	3.9	12.6
1983–84	5.5	13.0
1984–85	5.6	14.3
1985–86	8.7	13.5
1986–87	9.1	14.9
1987–88	7.3	15.7
1988–89	8.7	18.3
1989–90	8.3	15.95

Source: Different Issues of RBI Bulletin

This created a panic among investors and brokers and led to a prolonged closure of the stock exchanges along with a precipitous drop in share price.

7. Different committees highlighted the dominating role of brokers in the Governing Bodies which often hesitate to take strict disciplinary action against erring members indulging in excessive speculative activities.
8. When animal spirits dominate, rational behaviour withers, share price oscillates abnormally, market simply resembles casino that tempt investors to take a flyer in it. Table 3.6 distinctly shows that casino instincts dominated the market from 1985 to '92. This short span alone includes 29 positive and 24 negative changes in price in excess of ± 3% out of + 37 and –31 total changes for the entire period.
9. The government directed a large number of agencies namely, the Reserve Bank of India (RBI), the Central Bureau of Investigation (CBI), the Directorate of Income Tax Department, the Directorate of Enforcement, the Joint Parliamentary Committee (JPC) to investigate various aspects of the scam. This resulted in a chaotic situation and led to a prolonged closure of the market, eventuating abnormal drop in share price.
10. Substantial evidences show that, contrary to the efficient market hypothesis, news is not the only force driving asset prices. For example, Roll (1988) demonstrates that most idiosyncratic price moves in individual stocks can not be accounted for by public news. It is found that individual stocks exhibit significant price movements unrelated to the market on days when there are no public news, about these stocks. A similar and more dramatic result is obtained for the aggregate stock market by Culter, Poterba and Summers (1989), who find that the days of the largest aggregate market movements are not the days of most important fundamental news and vice versa. The present study shows a mixed evidence of 'noise' and 'news' in the abnormal price swings. The common conclusion of all these studies, is that news alone does not move share prices; noise trading by naive investors move them too.

REFERENCES

Cutler, David M., James M. Poterba, and Lawrence H. Summers, "What Moves Stock Prices?" *The Journal of Portfolio Management*, Spring 1989, No. 15, pp. 4–12.

Edwards, Franklin R. "Does Futures Trading Increase Stock Market Volatility?" *Financial Analysts Journal* (Jan.–Feb., 1988), pp. 63–69.

Fama, E.F. "Efficient Capital Market: A Review of Theory and Empirical Work", *Journal of Finance* (May 1970), pp. 383–47.

Greenwald, Bruce and Jeremy Stein. "The Task Force Report: The Reasoning Behind the Recommendations", *Journal of Economic Perspectives*, Vol. 2, No. 3 (Summer 1988), pp. 3–23.

Jensen, Michael C. "Some Anomalous Evidence Regarding Market Efficiency", *Journal of Financial Economics*, 6 (June–September 1978), pp. 95–102.

Jones, P. and W. Wilson. "Is Stock Price Volatility Increasing?" *Financial Analysts Journal* (Nov.–Dec. 1989), pp. 20–26.

Keynes, J.M. *The General Theory of Employment, Interest and Money* (1936), pp. 152–53.

LeRoy, S.F. and Porter, R.D. "The Present Value Relation: Test Based on Implied Variance Bounds." *Econometrica,* No. 49, pp. 555–571.

Roll, Richard R. "R-Squared", *Journal of Finance,* July 1988, 43, pp. 541–66.

Roll, Richard R. "The International Crash on October 1987", *Financial Analysts Journal,* September–October, 1988, pp. 19–35.

Schwert, G.W. "Why Does Stock Market Volatility Change Over Time?" *Journal of Finance,* Vol. XLIV, No. 5, (December 1989), pp. 1115–1153.

Schwert, G.W. "Stock Market Volatility", *Financial Analysts Journal,* May–June, (1990), pp. 23–24.

Shiller, R. "Do Stock Prices Move too much to be Justified by Subsequent Changes in Dividends?", *American Economic Review,* No. 71, (1981a). pp. 421–36.

Shiller, R. "The Use of Volatility Measures in Assessing Market Efficiency", *Journal of Finance,* No. 36, (1981b), pp. 291–304.

Wheeler, Langdou, B. "The Oscillation of Systems: The Missing Link Between Price Volatility and Market Efficiency", *Financial Analysis Journal* (July–August 1989), pp. 7–10.

CHAPTER IV

VOLATILITY AND MARKET EFFICIENCY

Throughout the unprecedented stock market boom of the 80's, there was a popular belief of excessive movement in share prices. The finding of the last chapter attests this perception when it reveals the case of excess volatility in the current period. Increased volatility *per se* can not be criticised if the price movement can be realistically explained by fundamental economic factors, otherwise it may strain the economy. Hence, the issues appear:

1. Can we trace the source of price movement in the recent time back in a logical manner to fundamental shocks affecting the economy? or,
2. Is price movement due to 'fads': waves of irrational optimism and pessimism, 'noise trading', 'feedback trading', or other market inefficiencies?

To investigate the above quarries, the plan of the study is designed as follows: some theoretical issues directly related with the test of market efficiency will be discussed in Section I. Empirical results of volatility test will be presented in Section II. Finally, in Section III we will interpret and conclude the findings of the study.

Section I: A Prelude to Empirical Studies

A simple model that is commonly used to interpret movements in share price index asserts that real stock prices equal the present value of rationally expected or optimally forecasted future real dividends discounted by a constant real discount rate. This valuation model is often used by economists and market analysts to provide plausible explanations for movements in stock price index. Thus, these movements by definition can be attributed to "new information" about future dividends. Mathematical representation of the above discussions may be stated in terms of the simple Efficient Market Model as follows:

According to the model, the real price P_t of a share at the beginning of the time period it is given by

$$P_t = \sum_{k=0}^{\alpha} y^{k+1} E_t D_{t+k} \qquad 0, 1 \ldots \quad (1)$$

where D_t is the real dividend paid at time t, E_t denotes mathematical expectation conditional on information available at time t, and y is the constant discount factor.

In Chapter II, we have developed the following efficient market model in terms of series as a proportion of the long-run growth factor λ^{T-t}, which has the effect of eliminating heteroscedasticity due to the gradually increasing size of the market

$$p_t = \sum_{k=0}^{\alpha} \bar{y}^{k+1} D_t d_{t+k} = E_t(p_t*) \qquad \ldots \quad (2)$$

where p_t is the real detrended stock price and

$$p_t^* = \sum_{k=0}^{\alpha} \bar{y}^{k+1} d_{t+k} = \bar{y}(p_{t+1}^* + d_t) \qquad \ldots \quad (3)$$

is a perfect foresight or *ex post* rational price.

We have deduced three variance inequalities for volatility comparison, which is the main thrust of the present study. The simplest inequality derived from model (2), puts a limit on the standard deviation of p_t in term of the standard deviation of p_t^*:

$$\sigma(p) \leq \sigma(p^*) \qquad \ldots \quad (I)$$

Other two inequalities have been derived from the model restated in innovation form which allows better understanding of the limits on stock price volatility imposed by the model. Thus the second inequality puts a limit on the standard deviation of the innovation in price δp in terms of the standard deviation of d:

$$\sigma(\delta p) \leq \sigma(d) / \sqrt{\bar{r}_2} \qquad \ldots \text{(II)}$$

and the third inequality puts a limit on the standard deviation of the change in price Δp in terms of standard deviation of d:

$$\sigma(\Delta p) \leq \sigma(d) / \sqrt{2\bar{r}} \qquad \ldots \text{(III)}$$

If the above three variance inequalities hold good in practice, the market can be designated as efficient, otherwise the existence of "fads" or "bubbles" in price can not be ignored.

Section II: Empirical Evidence

Using the equation $p_t^* = \bar{y}(p_{t+1}^* + d_t)$ and working backward from the terminal date we have determined p_t^* (p^* for 1991 was set at the average detrended real price over the sample) to compare volatility of detrended real price series p_t to the *ex post* rational price series p_t^*. Both p_t and p_t^* series are displayed in Figure 4.1.

Figure 4.1 shows a smooth and stable *ex post* rational price series p_t^* when compared with the actual volatile price series p_t. This behaviour of p_t^* is due to the fact that the present value relation relates p_t^* to a long-weighted moving average of dividends (with weights corresponding to discount factors) and moving averages tend to smooth the series averaged.

The elements of the inequalities (I), (II) and (III) are displayed in Table 4.1. Explanations of certain variables used for the inequality test are given below.

The long run exponential growth path is estimated from the relation $p_t = p_0(1+g)^t$ which may be written in terms of natural logarithm as

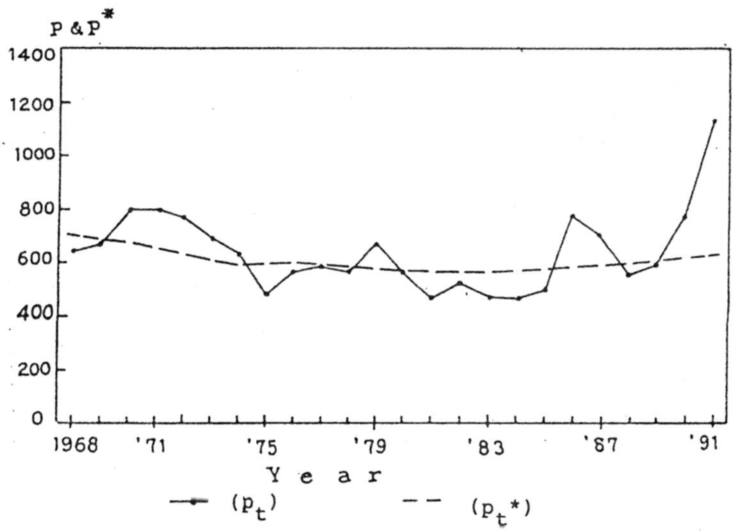

Fig. 4.1. Price (p) Volatility and Ex post Rational Price (p*) Variability

The solid line p_t is the real price series scaled by multiplying by $(1.00225)^{1991-t}$. The dashed line p_t^* is the ex post rational price series $[p_t^* = \bar{y}(p_{t+1}^* + d_t)$, where d_t is the real dividend detrended by multiplying by $1.00225^{1990-t}]$.

$$I_n p_t = I_n p_0 + tI_n (1 + g)$$

By regressing $I_n p_t$ on $I_n p_0$ and time t, it is easy to estimate $I_n(1+g)$or $I_n\lambda$. Then λ is set equal to e^b where b is the coefficient of time. The growth rate g is found to be 0.00225 i.e., 0.225 per cent over the period 1968 to 1991. This meager growth rate might be due to the fact that from mid-sixties to the beginning of eighties, the economy was suffering from stagflation.

The discount rate $\bar{r}$ (0.058451) used to compute p_t^* in (3) is estimated as the average d divided by the average p. The discount rate of 5.84 per cent may appear to be unrealistic at least in view of our present experience. However, it is the minimum average inflation adjusted rate of return of last 24 years from 1968 to 1991.

The terminal value of p* is taken as average p. If a different terminal condition is chosen, the result would be to add

Table 4.1. Sample Statistics for Price and Dividend Series

Sample Period	1968–1991
1. $E(p)$	639.7
$E(d)$	37.39
2. $\bar{r}$	0.0584
$\bar{r}_2$	0.1203
3. $b = I_n\lambda$	0.0022
$\hat{\sigma}(d)$	(0.2087)
4. $\sigma(d)$	12.4245
Elements of Inequalities	
Inequality (I)	
5. $\sigma(p)$	147.23
6. $\sigma(p^*)$	38.58
Inequality (II)	
7. $\sigma(\Delta p + d_{-1} - \bar{r}p_{-1})$	118.31
min (σ)	95.27
8. $\sigma(d)/\sqrt{\bar{r}_2}$	35.81
Inequality (III)	
9. $\sigma(\Delta p)$	119.27
min (σ)	96.61
10. $\sigma(d)/\sqrt{2\bar{r}}$	36.33

Note: In this table, E denotes sample mean, σ denotes standard deviation and $\hat{\sigma}$ denotes standard error. Min (σ) is the lower bound on σ computed as a one-sided $x^2$95 per cent confidence interval. The symbols p, d, $\bar{r}$, $\bar{r}_2$, λ and p^* have been defined in Table 2.1 of Chapter II. Data sets have also been mentioned under seperate heading of that Chapter. Inequality (I) in the text asserts that the standard deviation in row 5 should be less than or equal to that in row 6, inequality (II) that σ in row 7 should be less than or equal to that in row 8, and inequality (III) that σ in row 9 should be less than or equal to that in row 10.

or subtract an exponential trend from p_t^* shown in Figure 4.1. This is shown graphically in Figure 4.2, in which p_t^* was computed from alternative terminal values. Here also p_t^* remains smooth and stable as compared to the actual price series. As we move back from the terminal date, the deviation

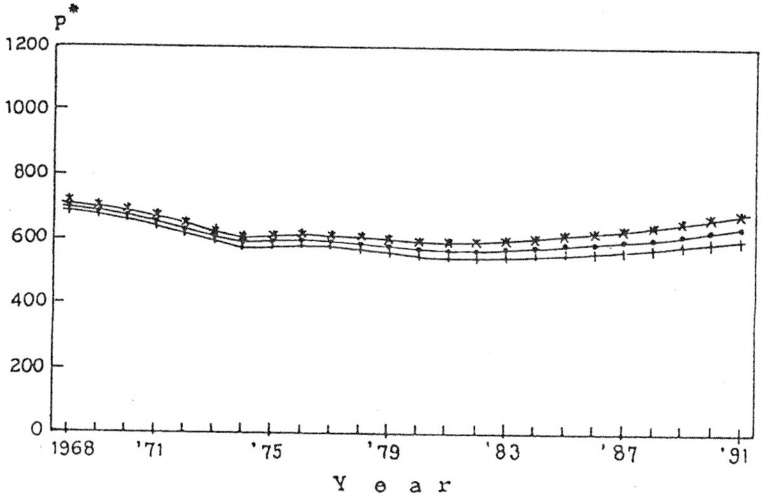

Fig. 4.2. Alternative Measures of Ex post Rational Price Series (p_t*)

between p_s* becomes minimum, hence the importance of the terminal value chosen declines.

Table 4.1 reveals that all inequalities are dramatically violated by the sample statistics. The left-hand side of the inequality is 3.3 to 3.81 times higher than the right hand side. The σ(d) over the entire sample was 12.42 while σ(Δp) was 119.97. The upper bound on the standard deviation of Δp allowed by the inequality (III) was thus (disregarding sampling error in the estimation of standard deviation) 36.33, so upper bound was exceeded by 3.3 times. Putting it another way, the standard deviation of d would have to be at least 41 in order to justify σ(Δp)[1]. Figure 4.3 gives an impression as to what extent price variation is being justified by the σ(d).

In Figure 4.3, Δp series ranges from –157.3 to 359.8, a range of over 4 standard deviations. The dashed lines mark of a ±2 standard deviation range from the mean μ (Δp) i.e., 25.90, where the standard deviation is σ = 36.33 or the upper bound allowed for σ(Δp) by inequality (III) given σ(d)= 12.42. So the area between the dashed lines is the maximum limit of the variation of (Δp), justified by the magnitude of σ(d). Thus the actual price volatility simply exceeds the level indicated by new information about the fundamental determinants of price.

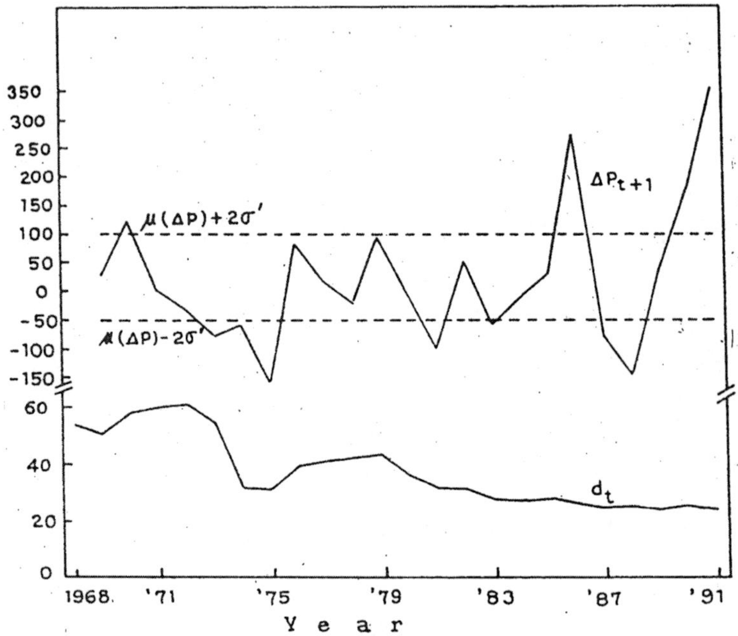

Fig. 4.3. Extent of Price Variation Explained by σ (d)

If Δp_t is assumed normal and serially uncorrelated, the lower bound of a 95 per cent one sided x^2 confidence interval for $\sigma(\Delta p)$ is 96.61, which is still over 2.6 times higher than the upper bound allowed by the measure of the observed variability of real dividend $\sigma(d)$. The lower bound thus so dramatically exceeds the limit allowed by the $\sigma(d)$ that it would seem impossible to attribute the excess volatility to such things as data errors, price index problems etc.

Volatility Test with a Revised Detrended Data Series

In the volatility test used here, the price and dividend data were detrended by an exponential decay factor (λ) to make them stationary. This method of detrending has become a source of controversy and most of the criticisms of the variance bounds inequality centred on this point (see Flavin, 1983; Marsh and Merton, 1984; Kleiden, 1986).

Taking cognizance of the above criticism, we revised the method of detrending in a different manner that depends only on past information (Shiller, 1984). The exercise was undertaken simply to substantiate that even if we adopt the revised methodology, the conclusion would remain unchanged.

Accordingly we have defined detrended price series P3, P5 and P7 and corresponding dividend series D3, D5 and D7 by

$$Pk_t = P_t / Nk_t \qquad k = 3, 5, 7$$

and $$Dk_t = D_t / Nk_t + P_{t-1}\left(\frac{1}{Nk_t} - \frac{1}{Nk_{t+1}}\right), \qquad k = 3, 5, 7$$

where Nk_t is a geometric moving average of lagged real earnings[2] and expressed mathematically as follows:

$$Nk_t = \pi_{j=1}^{k} \; E_{t-j}^{1/k} \qquad k = 3, 5, 7$$

Returns calculated with Pk and Dk in places of P and D in the formula for return r are the same as if P and D had been used. Thus, if equation (1) holds for P_t and D_t, then it holds where P_t and D_t are replaced by Pk_t and Dk_t and the same variance inequality of $\sigma(\Delta p) \leq \sigma(D)/(2\bar{r})^{1/2}$ should hold for Pk and Dk (Shiller, 1984).

Table 4.2 exhibits the elements of the above inequality, with the data detrended as above. The variables P3, P5 and P7 are the real stock price series detrended by the 3 year, 5 year and 7 year geometric average of lagged real earnings respectively. The Variables D3, D5 and D7 are the corresponding dividend series defined earlier. The constant $\bar{r}$ equals 0.05837, the average real return on the share price series over the entire period of 1968–1990.

The table reveals that the inequality is not violated for k=3 but when the value of k is extended to 5 and 7, the inequality is violated. When k increases from 5 to 7, $\sigma(\Delta P7)$ falls from 1.5692709 to 1.4003744, but the right hand side of inequality falls even further, from 0.933734 to 0.4121148, causing the inequality to be violated even more strongly.

Table 4.2. Sample Statistics for Revised Detrended Price and Dividend Series (1968–1991)

Sample Period	Left hand side of inequality	Right hand side of inequality
1972–1991	$\sigma(\Delta P3) = 1.6079347$	$\sigma(D3)/(2\bar{r})^{.5} = 1.8643301$
1974–1991	$\sigma(\Delta P5) = 1.5692709$	$\sigma(D5)/(2\bar{r})^{.5} = 0.933734$
1976–1991	$\sigma(\Delta P7) = 1.4003744$	$\sigma(D7)/(2\bar{r})^{.5} = 0.4121148$

The study clearly reveals that the share price volatility over the period 1968 to 1991 appears to be far too high to be attributed to new information about future real dividends. The movements of future dividend $\sigma(d)$ offer only a partial explanation of variation of price (Δp) and a considerable part of the price movement still remains unexpounded. The simple efficient market models which focus on rational fundamental factors only, fail to consider other subjective variables that may also influence share price movement.

Hence questions arise what is the alternative model of share price movement and how does it differ from traditional economic model? What are the variables ignored by economists that make their understanding about market behaviour imperfect? In the following section, we deal with the above investigation.

Section III: Interpretations and Conjectures

In the traditional economic view, each investor has a demand curve that slopes downward to the right. Lower stock prices result in more demand. The aggregate of individual demand curves also slopes downward to the right, but with a shallower slope. A given stock price change is associated with a larger change in demand than is the case with individual demand. Figure 4.4 illustrates the difference and the relationship between demand and supply when the supply of stock is assumed to be fixed.[3] In this case, the assumed shape of the demand curve assures that there will be a single equilibrium point, and that it will correspond to a reasonable price.

Given this model, changes in equilibrium price result through shifts in the demand curve. Figure 4.5 illustrates the process. Assuming the demand curve shifts horizontally,

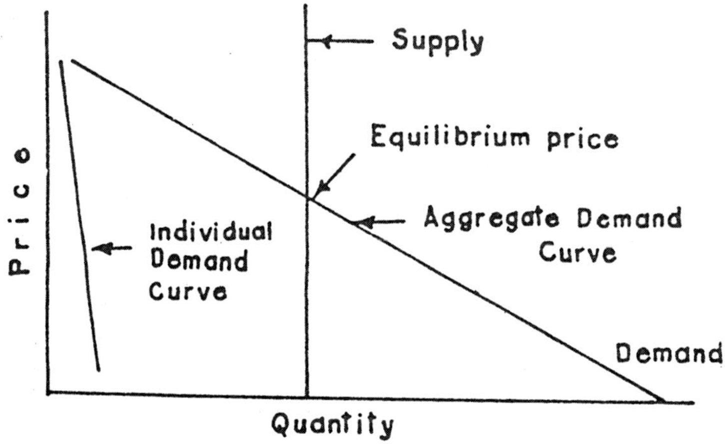

Fig. 4.4. Demand Curves with Fixed Supply

equilibrium price increases with a shift to the right and decreases with a shift to the left. Positive information about fundamentals alone results in a shift of the curve to the right while negative information can cause the curve to shift to the left. Extent of price changes through shift in the demand curve will of course depend upon the nature and importance of information relating to fundamentals arriving in the market.

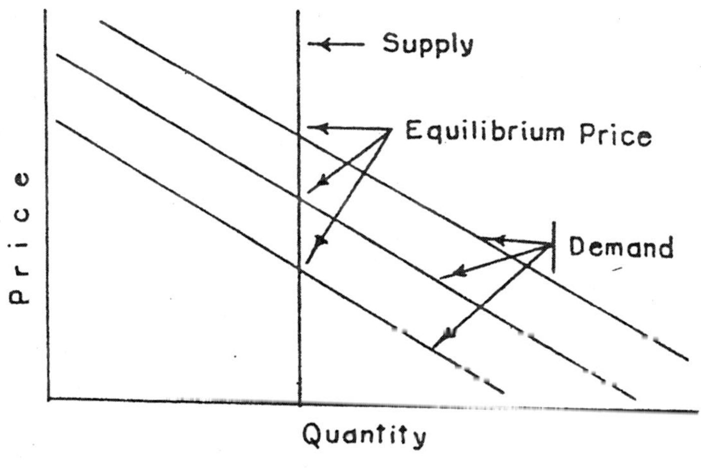

Fig. 4.5. Changes in Equilibrium

The market's continuity rests on two assumptions. The first is that the demand function is continuous in information and preference changes. The second is that the demand curve slopes downward to the right.

Traditional economic model of price formation seems inappropriate, as shift in demand very often results more from fashions and fads than that of change in the fundamentals. People under the influence of arbitrary elements buy when price rises and sell when it declines that further accentuate rise or fall in prices—the basic principle being "buy high & sell low". In the literature of finance this type of behaviour is often described as "extrapolative expectations about prices" or "trend chasing" (Frankel and Froot, 1986; Soro, 1987; Andreassen and Kraus, 1988). When investors chase trend, slope of the demand curve must move upward (see Figure 4.6). When price starts increasing, investors will then want to hold more stocks. But this is not possible being supply remains fixed. Their buy orders will simply increase the bid price and the higher bid price will lead to still more demand. Similarly when price starts declining, all investors will want to hold less stock, but their sell order will simply reduce the offer price, leading to still less demand (Ferguson, 1989), when shift in demand of investors, simply results from expectations based on extrapolations of past prices—prices that ultimately emerges can not be said as rationally determined (Case & Shiller, 1988).

Above is a simple description of price formation process in the stock market. Actual shape of the net demand curve as it is claimed by some researchers will depend upon the relative balance of "value based rational investors" and "naive" or "noise traders" in the market. Does rational value based investors really exist? Can they stabilize prices? This old question has been the subject of a large literature, dated back to Friedman (1953), Baumol (1957), Telser (1959), Farrell (1966), and Samuelson (1971) among others. Experiences of all earlier speculative episodes including the present one have a few lessons for us. First, investors by and large are not rational. Their demand for share depends much on their beliefs, sentiments and other arbitrary elements that are not fully

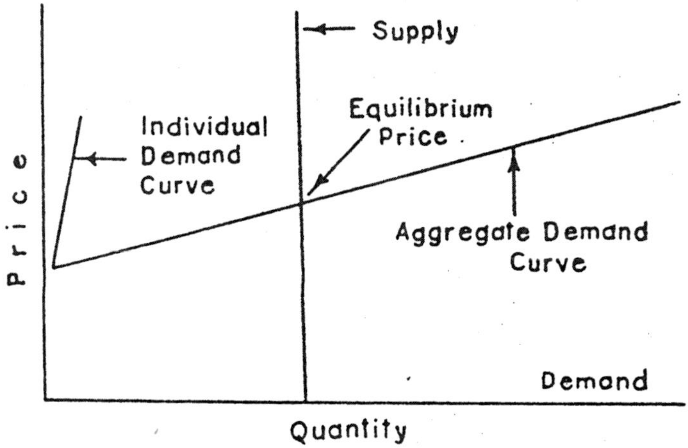

Fig. 4.6. Demand Curves of Alternative Apprcach

justified by fundamental news. Secondly even if "value based rational investors" exist their capacity and willingness to counter investors sentiment, thereby to stabilize price is not beyond suspicion (see Keynes, 1936; Shleifer and Summer, 1990).

Thus, there is the necessity to build models of financial equilibrium which are more sensitive to real life trading mechanisms, which account more realistically for the formation of expectations. Traditional economists busy with hard facts in their pursuit to describe boom and crashes completely ignore the role of fundamental psychological factors in the development of such unusual events of economy. It makes their understanding incomplete. We believe, along with hard economic factors, it is necessary to study the emotion, craze, belief, madness of individual and society at large that plays a none the less important role both in boom and crash. Any description that avoids the role of these subjective variables in formation of expectations is likely to be inconclusive, hence, it pays to develop economic models in the light of psychological knowledge.

Conclusion

The preceding chapter unveiled the fact of excessive price movement during the current period. The present chapter shows that this excess volatility can hardly be described by changes in fundamentals. A synoptic view that incorporates the roles of both objective and subjective variables in the price formation process has been illustrated to strengthen our knowledge about capital market behaviour.

In fact, the root of excessive volatility of current period may be traced both in and outside capital market. Ultimate victims of recent tragic episode is the genuine investors who suffered enormous loss in stock market operation. If disillusioned investors desert capital market *en masse* it would have a telling effect on much acclaimed programme of privatisation of Indian economy.

In view of the prevailing situation it becomes imperative to answer the following questions:

(a) Why should we care about market rationality?
(b) What are the implications of irrational behaviour of market for public policy?
(c) What steps have been taken so far to liberalise Indian financial system?
(d) Are the steps taken sufficient to improve the efficiency of the market?
(e) What is the impact of financial liberalisation on share price fluctuations?
(f) To what extent does the present behaviour of stock market impair the development process of our country?
(g) What role should the government play to safeguard the unerring investors against the preponderent influence of noise traders? and
(h) Finally, what remedial action should be initiated to make the market more efficient?

These are the issues to be discussed in the next chapter.

NOTES

1. Inequality (III) states that

$$\sigma(\Delta p) \leq \sigma d / \sqrt{2\bar{r}}$$

$$\text{or,} \quad \sigma(\Delta p) \cdot \sqrt{2\bar{r}} \leq \sigma d$$

$$\text{or,} \quad 119.97 \times \sqrt{2(0.0584)} \leq \sigma d$$

$$\text{or,} \quad 41 \leq \sigma d$$

2. The real earnings E_t is the average earnings for the calender year ending March, accruing to the portfolio represented by shares considered in the price series, divided by the average Wholesale Price Index of the respective year scaled to 1 in the base year 1991. Earning series have been collected from various issues of the Stock Exchange Official Directory, Bombay.
3. A feature of the stock market is that the total stock of shares is inelastic-the supply of new shares does not respond rapidly to changes in prices. Certainly, new issues of shares are made and directors of firms do tend to raise new capital or float their companies when share prices are high, but the response is not instant, partly because it takes times to prepare prospectuses, etc. When share prices seem to be low, companies may buy in more of their own shares and reduce the supply. Nevertheless, the supply of new shares is very much inelastic unlike the supply of any real asset. Hence the supply of shares is assumed to be fixed.

REFERENCES

Andreassen, Paul and Stephen Kraus. "*Judgemental Prediction by Extrapolation*", Harvard University Mimeo (1988).

Baumol, William J. "Speculation, Profitability and Stability" *Review of Economics and Statistics*, 39 (August 1957), pp. 263–71.

Case, Karl E. and Robert J. Shiller. "The Behaviour of Home Buyers in Boom and Post-Boom Market", *New England Economic Review* (Nov.–Dec. 1988), pp. 29–45.

Farrell, Michael J. "Profitable Speculation", *Economica*, 33 (May 1966), pp. 183–193.

Ferguson, Robert. "On Crashes", *Financial Analysts Journal* (March–April 1989), pp. 42–52.

Flavin, Marjorie A. "Excess Volatility in the Financial Markets: A Reassessment of the Empirical Evidence", *Journal of Political Economy*, Vol. 91 (December 1983), pp. 929–56

Frankel Jeffrey and Kennet Froot (1986). Explaining the Demand for Dollars: International Rates of Return and the Expectations of Chartists and

Fundamentalists in R. Chambers and P. Parrlberg eds. Agriculture, Macroeconomics and the Exchange Rate, Westfield Press, Boulder Co.

Friedman, Milton. *Essays in Positive Economics*, Chicago, University Chicago Press, 1953.

Keynes, J.M. *The General Theory of Employment, Interest and Money*. London: MacMillan, 1936, p. 157.

Kleidon, Allan W. "Variance Bounds Tests and Stock Price Valuation Models", *Journal of Political Economy*, 94 (October 1986), pp. 953–1001.

Marsh, A. and Robert C. Merton. "Dividend Variability and Variance Bounds Tests for the Rationality of Stock Market Prices", Working Paper 1584–84 (Massachusetts Institute of Technology, Alfred P. Sloan School of Management, August 1984).

Samuelson, Paul A. "Stochastic Speculative Price", *Proc. Nat. Acd. Sci.*, 68 (February 1971), pp. 335–37.

Shiller, R.J. "Stock Prices and Social Dynamics". *Brooking Papers on Economic Activity*, 2 (1984), pp. 457–498.

Shleifer, Andrei and Lawrence H. Summers. "The Noise Trader Approach to Finance", *Journal of Economic Perspectives*, Vol. 4, No. 2 (Spring 1990), pp. 19–33.

Soros, George. *The Alchemy of Finance*, Simon and Schuster, New York, 1987.

Telser, Lester G. "A Theory of Speculation Relating Profitability and Stability", *Review of Economics and Statistics*, 41 (August 1959), pp. 295–301.

CHAPTER V

SUMMING UP AND POLICY IMPLICATIONS

The present chapter attempts to summarise the main findings and conclude the study on *"Bubble: A Study of Scam, Scandal and Corruption in Indian Stock Market"*.

Broadly, the emphasis of the study was to investigate the following two research questions:

1. Is current level of volatility increasing?
   and
2. Can the present volatility be explained by fundamental economic factors?

In fact, the present study aims to measure and provide reasonable explanations of share price movement of Indian stock market.

Gamut of issues studied, would provide us an insight about the stock market behaviour of the present time, and the nature and extent of Capital Market reforms necessary to reach our economic destiny.

Section I: Findings of the Study

An upshot of empirical results reported in the study may be stated separately for the two hypotheses as follows:

To test whether current level of volatility is increasing, several measures of fluctuation based on different indices have been used. A glance at the study of monthly share price movements for a period 1935–1992 reveals that:

1. Overall standard deviation of monthly return for the complete period is 4.66685 per cent.

   Decadewise analysis, however, shows that violent changes in share prices cluster around the boom of 40s and share mania of 80s that continued up to 1992.
2. The entire period of 30 years from 1951 to 1980 may be treated as a period of low volatility.
3. Among the top 10 volatile years of the total period, 4 and 5 belong to boom of 40s and 80s respectively and only one outlying year is included in the tranquil period of the 70s.
4. 1992 stands out as the exceptionally volatile year of Indian stock market, and it is far ahead of 1946, the second in rank.

Even a cursory glance at the above findings, would unveil a trend of increasing share price fluctuation in the current period. The above conclusion is, however, based on monthly share price index. For a better understanding of price movement, it requires an indepth study based on daily share price index, that is available for a shorter period from 1961 to 1992. Volatility measured using daily share price index discloses the following:

1. Decadewise analysis of daily return for the period (1961 to 1992) displays that the decade 80s and the subperiod 1991–92 bear much higher standard deviations as compared to earlier decades.
2. 1992 stands out as the most volatile year followed by 1990 and 1986 as second and third respectively.
3. Out of 25 most volatile months for the entire period, only 2 belong to the calm period of 60s and 70s and the rest 23 pertain to the hectic period that started from 1980 and continued upto 1992. The distribution pattern of 23 months reveals a gradual increasing trend in market volatility that culminated in 1992 having as much as 7 months in its credit.
4. April 1992 comes out as the most volatile month (SD=3.23895%) followed by March 1992 (SD=3.17525%) and October 1990 (SD=2.7075%) as second and third respectively. Interestingly top 3 volatile months belong

to the most stormy period of Indian stock market that started from 1990.

5. Frequency distribution of 68 large price swings shows that the period 1990–92 alone shares as much as 31 spike changes followed by the second and the first half of 80s respectively.
6. Largest positive and negative daily price changes occurred on 2nd March (8.79802%) and 28th April (–6.82122%) of 1992. Interestingly the days belonged to the most successive volatile months of the highest volatile year.

Till now several volatility measures based on different share price indices have been used to evaluate the present stock price movement in historical perspective. In each instance, the conclusion is essentially the same. Drastic changes in share prices of the 40s were followed by a tranquil period of more than three decades and a tired look of price movement continued up to 1980. From the beginning of 80s, there was an indication of change in the present mood of the market. Ultimately volatility took a new shape from '85 and touched at the peak in 1992, suppressing all previous records.

After relative stability of three decades why did market volatility increase in the 80s? There are a number of plausible explanations to this question, that may even contradict with one another. Some may suggest that in the context of qualitative and quantitative changes in the stock market in the last few years, the greater volatility is nothing but the sign of improved maturity and higher efficiency of our capital market. Hence in this changing complexion, larger fluctuation can be explained by the fundamental economic factors. Others may simply blame 'noise' trading for the rise in volatility in the 80s. In order to search out the true explanation of the increased price movement, the study aimed to test the second hypothesis—"Present share price movement can be explained by Efficient Market Paradigm".

The evidence that is available from the study clearly reveals that the share price volatility over the period 1968 to 1991 appears to be far too high (3.3 to 3.81 times high) to be attributed to new information about future real dividends. If the rational expectation theory is correct, the movements of future dividend σ(d) justify a part of total variation of price (Δp). In a sense, the actual price volatility thus simply exceeds the level indicated by fundamental economic factors. The considerable part of the price movement which still remains unexplained, might be due to 'fads': waves of irrational optimism and pessimism, 'noise trading', 'feedback trading', or other market inefficiencies (Cochrane, 1991).

Information that is available so far particularly after unearthing of "Security Scam" reveals that outside finance often used by the noise traders for speculative business, along with other market imperfections, played a significant role behind the excessive fluctuation of share price. Blessed with public money, the noise traders, in fact, dominated market in those days, and over-powered information traders when trading against them belying the hope of Friedman on arbitrage operation (Friedman, 1953).

The outweighing noise traders thus simply destabilize the market and move security prices away from fundamentals, resulting in 'fads' or bubbles' as the natural outcomes in the price formation process.

In view of the prevailing situation, it becomes imperative to answer the following questions:

1. Why should we care about excessive fluctuation of share price?
2. What are the implications of irrational behaviour of market for public policy?

Section II: Economic Implications of Excessive Fluctuations

Development of an efficient financial system capable to provide array of services to the rest of the economy is an essential condition for successful economic reform. The market can discharge its allocative function efficiently only when price reflects fundamentals well and extent of price changes simply depends upon the nature and importance of news relating to fundamentals arriving in the market. Alternatively, if the price is 'noise' driven instead of 'news' driven, then the confidence of economists in the efficiency of market allocations of investment resources is, to say the least, weakened. This is often referred to as market failure, as the competitive market is failing to bring about an efficient allocation of resources. Thus the present section devotes solely to study the economic implications of excessive share price fluctuation.

Savings Mobilization

Mobilization of savings and distribution of funds for productive use are two basic functions of the finance system. Excessive gyration in share price due to abrupt shift in the perception of risk and return of noise traders through asset that is not subject to any fundamental uncertainty introduces additional risk in equity investment that may seriously threaten the fund mobilizing capacity of the market. This additional risk created by noise traders may compel genuine investors to desert stock market leaving it as a domain of speculators alone.

Resource Allocation

If corporate sector ultimately has to revert to old means of financing by banks this may make financial liberalisation attempt difficult. From the time of Adam Smith, economists have extolled the virtues of the competitive price system as a mechanism for allocating scarce resources. The free operation of the competitive market can be shown to result in a Pareto optimal allocation of capital provided information processing function of a competitive market has optimal property. But in many occasions, the fads in the pricing system belies the above claim of the economists. Noisy price movements impart pseudosignal to investors regarding efficiency of the firm which indulges in misallocation of scarce resources of the society. When people realise the ills of misallocation of resources, cost of shifting capital within and between sectors prevents them from doing so, ultimately economy suffers.

Corporate Governance

In market economies large private firms are typically owned by a dispersed group. For obtaining and analyzing information about firms is time consuming and costly, firm owners frequently know less than their managers about how their firms work. But managers may have interests different from those of shareholders and may act in their own interests instead of maximising the long run value of the firm. Market economies have developed a number of mechanisms for the purpose. Some involve aligning the interests of principal with those of the agent by trying management compensation to the value of the firm. Reliance on the stock market to align the interests of management and owners requires the market to reveal information about the firm efficiently. The market through continuous adjustment of stock prices—can assist in monitoring managers of publicly traded corporations, thereby possibly improving corporate governance. A market whose destiny is totally guided by unscrupulous speculators can not at least generate reliable information about management.

Distribution of Wealth

Economists feel safe (Fama, 1965; Friedman, 1956) to ignore the role of irrational investors in asset price formation. Underlying assumption is, in the long run wealth is redistributed from investors with inferior information to those with better information, thus irrational investors will lose money and eventually disappear from the market. However, this intuitively appealing explanation loses its significance when market weighes traders information by wealth not by quality. A trader with inferior information but large wealth may have his information overvalued in the market and market will be inefficient. Dubious role of outside finance to strengthen the money power of erring speculators and its impact on the Indian capital market was the subject matter of attention of many government appointed committees. Irrational investors simply by money power supplied by outside agencies very often outperform information trader that results in a redistribution of wealth from information to noise traders that also ensures noisy price in the market. Imperfect distribution of wealth obviously has a welfare implication, when welfare is computed with respect to correct distribution of return.

Section III: Significance of Stock Market in an Efficient Financial System

A financial system that functions well requires that the whole financial sector functions efficiently. There can be important relations among the various financial institutions and complementarities from the point of view of capital suppliers and demanders. The ill-functioning stock market may limit the ability of firms to achieve an efficient mix of debt and equity, in spite of a well functioning debt market. In this sense, stock markets and other financial intermediaries may function as complements, rather than substitutes and a stock market that functions well may have positive externalities for the rest of the financial system.

Unfortunately efforts to improve the functioning of financial markets of developing countries, that is, to allocate capital more efficiently, have often focussed only on core financial theme such as interest liberalisation, smaller government role in credit allocation and improvement in the role of banks as financial intermediaries. Undenyingly in many LDCs, banking sector is the only organised capital market, equity market either does not exist or it is so ill developed that it performs a barely useful role in the economy. Most presumably this fact has inspired theorists to concentrate on banking sector alone in isolation of equity market while describing the role of liberalised financial system in the development process of LDCs.

The literature on financial liberalisation has emphasised the desirability of a market oriented financial policy in order to raise domestic saving and improve the allocative efficiency of capital. It has neglected the role of equity markets for efficient capital allocation and risk sharing in a liberalised financial environment. But the important question arises—whether full scale liberalisation of the banking sector alone is sufficient to achieve the allocative efficiency of capital, given the current structure of equity markets. Cho (1986) examines the issue and concludes that liberalisation of the banking sector would not achieve efficient capital allocation in the absence of wellfunctioning equity markets. It is suggested that substantial development of an equity market is a necessary condition for complete financial liberalisation. To quote Cho, "In a credit market with imperfect information, liberalisation of the banking system . . . would not, by itself, be sufficient to achieve full efficiency . . . . This is due to the adverse selection effect (and also the moral hazard effect) that occurs when delet contracts are used in the presence of asymmetric information . . . . Equity contracts, however, are free from adverse selection effects and could thus overcome inefficient allocation of capital when the same degree of imperfect information on borrowers exists as in the case of debt contracts" (Cho 1986, p. 198).

The importance of a well developed equity market in a deregulated financial system of LDCs are: first, the financial services and institutions fostered by equity markets are important complements to bank funding and retained earnings in financing investment; second, equity market which is free from adverse selection and moral hazard effect can allocate resources more efficiently than bank constrained with imperfect information (Cho, 1986), third, existence of risk-bearing capital in the system may help to reduce concentration of risk in monetary institution (Snowden, P.N. 1987).

The importance of the equity market mentioned above, in fact, has started being recognised since the beginning of the 80s. Many LDCs which until quite recently had highly regulated financial market, felt strongly that a new precept based on the past knowledge and contempory experiences of other nations to be adopted to successfully meet the growing capital needs associated with growth and development. This new precept was financial deregulation that swept swiftly over many LDCs during 80s. The shift in the policy opened a new vista for the development of equity market which was greeted with enthusiasm both by domestic and overseas investors. Belying the assumptions of Mckinnon (1973) and Shaw (1973), now-a-days equity markets of these countries are successfully complementing bank funding and retained earning for the development of corporate sector. Although there are conflicting (mixed) results of the Financial Liberalisation, there is almost a unanimity among the academics that liberalisation encourages the formation of equity markets where they did not previously exist, and help in their deepening where predated the reforms. Indeed, recently there has been a proliferation of scholarly and popular articles which extol the virtues of these rapidly expanding markets for LDC economic performance and for investors world wide.

The expansion of equity markets of many Asian countries specially after liberalisation is truly impressive (see Appendix E). The market capitalisation of these countries continue to grow. Some of these emerging markets are comparable in size to the smaller European markets and many of them have been growing at a faster rate than European markets over the last few years and are likely to continue to do so.

However, all these encouraging developments in the emerging markets have been largely overshadowed by excessive fluctuation of share prices (see Appendix F). The phenomenon contradicts the assumption of financial liberalisation hypothesis that predicts a decrease in volatility following liberalisation and discount its microeconomic effect. In fact, whether and to what extent expanded stock markets are a boon or impediment to real sector growth and stability in LDCs largely depends in part on the level of volatility they exhibit. Markets with frequent and severe price swings might be much more prone to induce short term speculative investment practices and might also be more likely to lead to financial crisis and misallocation of savings and investment to the detriment of real sector growth and stability (Ilene Grabel 1995). Major international institutions, satisfied with the fascinating growth of emerging markets also expressed their concern repeatedly over the unusual behaviour of these markets.

The encouraging development in the emerging markets has allured Indian policy makers to involve a regime shift[1] from highly regulated (1951–80) to gradually deregulating financial system (1981–92) on the functioning of capital market. In fact almost from the beginning of 80s, government gradually initiated some measures which are fundamental to financial liberalisation, such as, hike in the rate of interest on debenture, relaxation and subsequent abolition of Monopoly and Restrictive Trade Practice Act (MRTP), introducing new instruments, development of new institutions, widening and deepening the activities of existing institutions, abolition of controller of capital issues department, offering more liberties to private sector for timing and pricing of new issues, greater freedom to banks over their portfolio, revision of interest rate structure etc. The following section clearly mentions the different steps already taken to liberalise Indian financial system. This would help us to see how these measures helped to activate the capital market. The experiences of many LDCs show that liberalisation induces increase in share price volatililty. The lessons from Indian market will further contribute in our understanding the relationship between financial liberalisation and asset price fluctuation and its impact on LDC economies.

Section IV: Financial Sector Reforms—Steps and Implication

The reform policies so far ventured by the government are fundamental to the goals of liberalisation. The essence of this change is that where market can function best, decision should be left to it.

The recent moves by the government to develop a market oriented financial system may be broadly classified into six categories. It shows that the government is determined to implement its avowded objectives of deregulation with a caution so as to avoid the problems that sudden financial decompression has created in many Latin American countries. In fact, gradual deregulation and a policy of close supervision by Monetary authorities over the financial system so as to minimise the scope of distortions during the change process are the two principles that the government is following meticulously. The steps taken so far will further reveal that the process of development of a market oriented financial system is still in progress and due to slow process several more years will be necessary to reach the target. Some measures taken so far to liberalise Indian financial system are:

1. *Deregulation of Price, Interest Rate etc.*

— Gradual deregulation of interest rates in the banking system while a minimum lending rate and maximum deposit rate remain.
— Freeing call money and almost all other rates of interest in the money market.
— Interest rate of Government securities are increasingly being related to markets.
— Free pricing of shares subject to certain restrictions.

2. *Autonomy to Public Sector Banks*

— Strengthening capital base of public sector banks through direct budgetary support and changes in legislation enabling them to mobilise resources from the market.
— Forced holdings of government securities by commercial banks have been reduced.
— Subsidized credit to priority sector has been rationalised.
— Control over banks lending decisions have been relaxed.
— The Cash Reserve Ratio (CRR) on incremental deposits and Statutory Liquidity Ratio (SLR) has been reduced.

3. *Privatisation of Institutions to Increase Competitiveness*

— Private sector banks are allowed to operate in the economy.
— Private sector mutual funds are permitted to function in the capital market.
— Foreign banks are allowed to participate in the equity of new private banks with some restrictions.

4. *Deregulation of International Transactions*

— Foreign institutional investors have been allowed to operate in Indian capital markets.
— Country funds have been established, the proceeds of which being invested in Indian stock market.

5. *Institution Building and Improvement of Infrastructure*

- Securities Trading Corporation of India has been set up to provide liquidity for dated government securities.
- Discount and Finance House of India Limited (DFHIL) has been established to activate secondary market for the money market instruments.
- Securities and Exchange Board of India (SEBI) has been established to act as a regulatory agency for the capital market in India.
- Over the counter market (OTC) and unlisted Securities market (USM) have been developed to provide liquidity to secondary market.
- The inauguration of the National Stock Exchange of India (NSE) with an exclusive trading floor for transparent and screen based trading in all types of debt instruments.
- Agency to facilitate credit rating has been established (CRISIL).

6. *Integration of Capital and Money Market*

- Permission granted to banks to diversify their activities into para banking areas like merchant banking, mutual funds, leasing, venture capital, credit rating etc.
- Non-bank financial institutions are permitted to operate in the call money market.
- Banks are now permitted to extend loans against shares and for share brokers.

Action taken so far to liberalise Indian financial system clearly shows that a number of measures have already been taken by the government to improve the functioning of equity market. The steps mentioned above are not exhaustive but indicative. The important point to mention is that the development role of the equity market has been righty recognised and steps have been taken to improve its efficiency along with the banking sector. Objective is to achieve full efficiency of capital allocation through developing an integrated financial system essential for the success of financial liberalisation.

Reaction of the Market

Thanks to financial liberalisation, Indian stock market like many other Asian markets also experienced stupendous growth in the recent time (see Table 5.1). Slowly but steadily it is complementing bank funding for the development of corporate sector. Ironically this market also suffers from the menace of overspeculation and excessive price fluctuation, which is in fact, more fierce than many of its counterparts.

The two related main issues that have been examined in this study are the extent of volatility and the information content of prices. Most specifically the first issue relates to the question of whether current level of volatility in share price is increasing. The evidence of higher volatility[2] gives rise to the second and related issue that concerns to the question of whether short-term volatility of stock price is 'excessive' in the sense that it is greater than that in the underlying fundamentals relating to corporate profits, dividend payments and interest rates. The evidence of 'excessive' volatility[3] gives rise to another related issue of the information content of prices, and the possibility of speculative bubbles. The greater the existence of bubble the less informative is the price system, and hence the greater magnitude of noise. The excessive volatility is thought likely to lead to a weakening of investor confidence, thus discouraging participation of risk-neutral and risk-averse investors and contributing to a vicious cycle. The noisy price also misallocates the scarce resources and the market loses its economic significance. These vices are sufficient to defeat the basic purpose of financial liberalisation where society in effect authorizes the financial system to mobilize and allocate resources efficiently.

Relationship between Liberalisation and Price Fluctuations

The key assumption of financial liberalisation hypothesis is, the reform would help to decrease overall volatility of the stock market by increasing the numbers of both investors and tradeable shares, encouraging the increased production and dissemination of reliable information, developing new

Table 5.1. Key Indicators of the Growth Pattern of Indian Stock Market, Pre and Post Liberalisation Period

	Period of Mixed Economy (1961–79)	Period of Real Sector Reform (1980–90)		Financial Sector Reform					
		1980	1890	'91	'92	'93	'94	'95	'96
No. of stock exchanges	7	9	19	20	21				23
No. of listed companies	1203	2265	5969	6229	6480	6800			
Market value of listed equity capital (Rs. in crores)	1292	6750	70521	110279	354106	NA	NA	NA	250509
Estimated number of share owning individuals (Lakhs)	6.25	24	NA	60	200	NA	NA	NA	NA
Average turnover (Rs. in crores)			36012	71777	45695	84536	67740	50064.94	NA
Capital raised by private sector (Rs. in crores)	98.92	195.77	2160.37	6193.1	19825.6	2994.80	NA	NA	NA
Resource mobilisation by Mutual Funds (Rs. in crores)					13021	11243	11275	NA	NA

Source: *The Stock Exchange Official Directory*, Bombay, 1993

institutions, writing and enforcing laws and prudential regulations, training financial specialist etc. (Ilene Grabel 1995). In a sense, it is assumed that financial deepening would contribute in the maturity of the market by sharpening the link between information and market outcome that would ultimately prevent irrational movement of share price.

From a Keynesian perspective, however, quickened pace of financial transactions following liberalisation may be expected to contribute to higher volatility which is in effect self-nourishing. Volatility forces investors to shorten their time horizons for both offensive (profit seeking) and defensive (loss minimising) reasons, with the paradoxical effect of inducing increased volatility. It implies that increases in market volatility in post liberalisation period may lead to reductions in real sector investment activities.[4]

Table 5.2 shows the share price volatility of Pre and Post Liberalisation period.[5] As shown in the table, the regime of suppressed financial system (pre liberalisation period), was the tranquil period of the Indian stock market. The price fluctuation for the entire period was below long range average. Bidding farewell to "Control regime", Indian economy gradually entered into an era of liberalisation from 80s. A shift in the balance in the economy from state to the private sector demands reform of capital market to meet the growing capital need of corporate sector. Immediately after the regime shift, the stock market started booming, but gyration of share price increased belying the hope of financial liberalisation theorists.

Table 5.2. Volatility of Monthly Return: Pre and Post Liberalisation Period

Time period	n	% Mean	% SD
Pre Liberalisation			
1961–1980	5107	0.015641552	0.519818668
Post Liberalisation			
1981–1990 (period of real sector reform)	2319	0.0667936	1.002394
1991–1995 (period of financial sector reform)	1097	0.09470204	1.31294988
All	8523	0.039721643	0.811240817

The extremely volatile market during the boom followed by crash raises the question regarding whether and to what extent, the market buoyancy was a boon or impediment to real sector growth and stability of the economy. The following section will address the issue with a view to highlight its impact on real economy.

Section V: Development Implications

Buoyancy continued till March 1992. Carefree investors, in those days, were excited with the fabulous rates of return, the government was jubilant with incredible fund mobilizing capacity of the market and market authorities were proud with the changing image and increasing importance of stock market in the national economy. Virtually the government spared no opportunity to adore the contribution of new economic policy for the current salutary state of the market.

Of course, there were reasons for complacency. Bullish investors who misperceived expected return overinvested in stocks during price rise. Their enthusiasm ushered liquidity in an otherwise illiquid market, the phenomenon that was seriously impending new investment for long. Eventually there was a shift in the flow of funds from nonproductive to productive asset. All these inspiring developments in the capital market prompted mushroom growth of new industries and there was havoc increase in the number of listed companies in all the stock markets.

Thus economy was enormously benefitted by the growing supply of funds for productive use and wealth increased during this short span to an extent that was satisfactory. The government expected if this casino instincts of market would continue for few more years; it would lead to success of new industrial policy and bring us to economic eldorado where all our reasonable economic needs would be satisfied (Keynes, 1931).

In fact, irrational behaviour of investors cuts both ways. Once considered as blessing, it suddenly proved as a curse for the economy soon after 1992–93 budget when the news of security scandal poured in the society. Scandal once again[6] unveiled shady nexus between speculators and outside money particularly public money to strengthen activities of noise traders. The extent of outside financing can easily be guessed from the available information that reveals misappropriation of funds to the tune of over Rs. 5000 crores from bank and other public sector units. The erring speculators thus blessed with public money outperformed information traders in those days both in number and wealth that resulted in a redistribution of resources from information to noise traders. The process continuously rewarded irrational and punished rational investors that ultimately ensued noisy price[7] in the market (Figlewski, 1978).

Blemish redistribution of wealth was followed by inefficient allocation of scarce resources. Noisy price led investors to misallocate resources and funds were in fact available in plenty to all industries irrespective of their intrinsic worths. Thus benefits that were expected to accrue to the economy during buoyancy, were largely offset by misutilization of scarce resources.

In fact, misery of indulging irrational behaviour was prominent when bubble burst. Investors soon realized that they have the asset with negative present value that is difficult to transfer to any buyer without incurring enormous capital loss. Banks and other public sector units that financed noise traders, not only suffered a serious setback but their role in the whole episode also evoked severe criticism.

The government's liberalization policies came under harsh criticism after the 'meltdown', and bowing to the political pressures and the bad press they received during the stock market tragedy, these policies were put on hold for a while by the government. The Securities and Exchange Board of India (SEBI) postponed sanctioning of private sector mutual funds. Implementation of some aspects of the recommendations by Narasimham Committee on the banking system was also delayed. Questions were raised regarding privatization of public sector enterprises. The much talked about entry of foreign pension funds and mutual funds became more remote than ever. The Euro-issues planned by several Indian companies were delayed since the ability of Indian companies to raise equity capital in the world markets was severely compromised. Supply of new funds from domestic market also

Table 5.3. Capital Issues, Quarterly Review of 1992

Quarter	Rs. in crores
January–March	2093.3
April–June	2904.8
July–September	1024.1
October–December	not available

Source: The Economic Times, Calcutta, 5 October 1992

started drying up and industries as usual mounted pressure on the government to underwrite new issue. The government through experiences soon realized that market can not be equated with casino having no relation with outside economy and there was fanatic attempt to overcome gloom.

Section VI: Major Problems of the Market

The foregoing discussion clearly indicates that equity market has a positive role for the real sector of the economy, provided the market functions efficiently. In fact, during the boom the economy benefited from the increasing fund mobilising capacity of the market, but it was largely offset by the misallocation of scare resources, i.e., the unavoidable outcome of imperfect functioning of the market. Before prescribing remedial measures to improve the market efficiency, it is needed to identify properly the cronic problem of the market. In view of the fact this section attempts to identify the major perennial problems of the Indian stock market.

A. Excessive Speculation

> "Speculators may do not harm as bubbles on a steady stream of enterprise. But the position is serious when enterprise becomes the bubble on a whirlpool of speculation. When the capital development of a country becomes a by-product of the activities of a casino, the job is likely to be ill-done."
>
> *(Keynes, 1931)*

Keynes' perception of excessive speculation completely dominated the Indian stock market during the 80s and early 90s. The casino instincts of the market confirms that the central weakness of the market is the existence of unhealthy and excessive speculation resulting in irrational price behaviour and high volatility. The overspeculative character of the Indian stock market is reflected from the fact of "share trading velocity"[8] that states the ratio of shares traded in the market to all shares outstanding. A comparison of such velocity with that in other countries as shown below can give an idea whether and to what extent the speculation is excessive.

A comparative analysis of the BSE with NYSE (see appendix G) brings out that trading in Bombay was concentrated in a small fringe of the market, whereas the trading in New York was more widely distributed. The trading velocity of individual shares in BSE were much higher than that of NYSE. An examination of trading concentration in terms of percentage of trading volume also indicates to the speculative dominance of India stock market.

B. Lack of Liquidity

Indian stock market is extremely narrow and limited and lacks substantial breadth. A large percentage of listed securities are either traded infrequently, or not at all, with volumes concentrated on a relatively few number of scrips, particularly of the long established and well managed companies (see Appendix H). As a result, a genuine investment buyer is not able to find a ready seller in the market for a majority of shares and vice versa. Trading concentrated to a limited number of blue chip shares, very often, commends market prices that reflect more often their scarcity value than their intrinsic worth resulting in 'fads' or 'bubbles' as the natural outcomes.

C. Insider Trading

Another major problem of the market is rampant insider trading[9] that is one of the principal causes of excessive speculative activity leading to violent price fluctuation. It is common knowledge in the market that some of the persons connected with industrial houses and top executives of the companies, including their directors, frequently trade in shares of their own company or group companies. To establish healthy trade practice in the stock exchanges and to sustain the confidence of the investors, such insider trading should be regulated by law. However, no comprehensive legislation to regulate insider trading is framed as yet in our country.

D. Outside Finance

As already pointed out, outside finance often used by the noise traders for speculative business, played a significant role behind the excessive price movement. It is observed that the main attraction in providing such finance for speculative transactions in shares is the lucrative rate of interest and availability of better margin of easily realisable securities. Such finance, being of a short term nature, while enabling the operators to take temporary delivery of shares from the markets, often lands the operators into serious financial difficulties if it is withdrawn suddenly for any reason, obliging the operators to liquidate their position prematurely. Hence, provision of outside finance by giving impetus to excessive speculation activity in some of the leading stock exchanges, exercises a baneful and destabilising influence on the trading activity in the stock exchanges.

E. Other Factors Contributing to Price Fluctuation

The other factors infusing to excessive volatility are:

(a) Increasing participation of local and foreign institutional investors (specially after liberalisation) in an essentially narrow market.
(b) Inadequate rules and regulations to control insider trading, market rigging, and to curb the role of outside money to finance carry over transactions.
(c) Lack of timely and proper disclosure of sufficient corporate information.
(d) Lack of effective machinery for reporting, monitoring, inspection and audit of market operations.

(e) Wide spread abuses of exchange rules and hesitancy on the part of the governing bodies to deal with crisis situation promptly, firmly and impartially.

The foregoing review of the problems of Indian stock markets leads to the conclusion that excessive speculation on the stock exchanges is the root cause of frequent crisis and consequent disruption of trading activities and distortion of price structure. Different committees have also viewed that the offences such as insider trading, non-delivery of scrips, short sales beyond a reasonable limit, non reporting or misreporting of transaction by brokers, Kerb trading, outside finance, often by way of indulging speculation result in wide fluctuation in the share price. The recklessly speculative condition has become the rule rather than exception in every historical bubble including the recent one. When the bubble bursts, investors lose confidence in the market. They begin to see financial markets as the provinces of the speculators and insiders only not of rational long term investors. When this view becomes pervasive, the investors get duped and lose their confidence and simply withdraw from the market (Edward 1988).

Should the government do anything to protect the interest of unerring investors to restore their confidence and to improve efficiency of the market? There are, however, divergence of opinion among academic economists regarding desirability of government intervention in the operation of the market—that varies from complete banning of speculative transaction at one extreme to "no intervention" on the other. The ultimate decision will, of course, depend upon social welfare function.

Complete ban on forward trading, is very often considered by the policy makers as the easiest means to get rid of the ills of overspeculation. But such a prohibition for an indefinite period can hardly be justified, as the social cost of banning may outweigh its benefit. In absence of forward trading, there will be little transaction in security, market would become captive and fail to ensure price continuity, liquidity, and fair evaluation of scrips.[10] Such developments may force investors to stay out of the market; and the market being devoid of blessings of investors, will lose its economic significance.

In favour of "no intervention" at all in the operation of the market there is one school which opines that we often allow people to participate in state lotteries, to lose fortunes in casinos or to bet on the racetrack even though benevolent observers know that they are being taken to cleaners. The case for making it costly for investors to bet on the stock market to protect them from their own utility losses is in principle identical to the case for prohibiting casinos, horse races etc. But this intuitively appealing "no intervention" argument loses its significance in view of the fact that, unlike a casino the financial markets are inextricably linked with the world outside, and the real economy pays the price for its dysfunctioning (De Long et al., 1989).

Ideally one would like to find an optimum solution that cripples destabilising noise while leaving untouched the ability of asset markets to fulfil their resource allocation and liquidity providing functions. Although a certain volume of speculation is needed to maintain market liquidity and efficient pricing, excessive speculation or trading on insider information can be destabilising, particularly in a situation with regulated financial system (see Dailami and Atkin 1990). In the financial system with controls on credit and interest rates, a liberalised stock market can act as a conduit for speculative pressures that would otherwise be released elsewhere. This suggests that efficient stock market development be accompanied by liberalization of the financial sector; it is also important to follow prudent macroeconomic policies. The government has already initiated financial sector reforms in India and fortunately the macroeconomic conditions now seem to be more or less stable. Action taken so far to liberalise Indian financial system clearly reveals that a number of measures have already been taken by the government to improve the functioning of equity market. With the rapid implementation of new policy perspective, the operations of the market have started showing significantly more efficiency. There still may arises questions: Whether the steps taken so far to regulate the capital market are adequte to ensure a reasonable level of speculation and to restore the confidence of the investors? If not, what additional measures may be initiated to improve further the efficiency of the equity market? These are the issues to be addressed in the next sections.

Section VII: Policy Implications

An well functioning financial system is essential for successful transformation of older economies towards dereguation, liberalisation, privatization and above all globalisation. Like many other developing countries India also rightly persuaded a number of steps to develop its equity market to achieve its avowed objective of economic liberalisation. Unfortunately, excessive speculation and riotious share price movement shows that capital market reform programme already initiated by the government though praisworthy but not sufficient to ensure "constrained parato-efficient allocation of resources" in the sense developed by DIXIT etc. In fact, the chronic problems of the market still remain there and to some extent it fails to ensure the 'Market Discipline'. The most worrying problem about trading in Indian stock exchanges is that it is ever crisis-prone due to its speculative rather than investment orientation. It is, therefore, felt that there is still room for further measures to be undertaken to prevent the market from excessive speculation and to help it be investment oriented and thereby to improve pricing efficiency. We therefore, prescribe the following corrective measures to be initiated by the authorities concerned to reform the capital and money market with a view to restore the lost confidence of domestic investors and also to invite the attention of offsore investors to our market. If the capital market can sustain its efficiency then only industries depending on their merit, can raise the required resources directly from the market, relieving the government from the burden of funding corporate sector-which is the essence of the new economic policy.

1. *On Structural Reforms*

The efficient organisational structure is a pre-requisite condition for an efficient functioning of the market. Hence, we propose a uniform organisational structure among all the stock exchanges having democratic representation of different interest groups. It would facilitate to deal with crisis situation promptly, firmly, and impartially and to take strict disciplinary action unhesitatingly against erring members indulging in excessive speculative activities.

2. *On Improvement of Operational Efficiency*

Security markets around the world are considering changes in their modus operandi that provides high level of liquidity and efficient price discovery. In this pursuit steps to be initiated may include enhancement of trading hours, reduction of settlement as well as carryforward period, demarcation of trading session between settlement and cash business, strict regulations for settlement transaction, advancement of computerised trading and development of communication system etc.

Maintenance of the operational efficiency, however, largely depends upon the prudent use of available mechanisms such as imposition of margin money, volume restriction, transfer of shares from specified to cash list etc., to control the temporal disequilibrium of the market. The market authority must develop a professional approach for the judicial implementation of the said mechanisms as and when required. Along with these measures, strict vigilance to curb the menance of 'option trading', 'kerb trading' and 'insider trading' is also essential.

Experience shows in the recent debacle, insitutional failure—inability of the government to restructure and reform the existing system contributed equally with the imperfection of internal structure of market.[11] In fact, the similar view was echoed while the government had attributed the reason for the scam to "system failure".

Hence we suggest the policies to be followed by the government to immune the market from occurrence of such unwarranted events in future.

3. *On Building up to Regulatory Environment*

A number of measures may be undertaken to ensure a regulatory environment. These measures include instituting legal provisions to prohibit insider trading and the means to enforce them, improving accounting and reporting standards and ensuring efficient disclosure of price sensitive information.

(a) Development of legal and regulatory environment
Legal and regulatory environment must be conducive to deal firmly and promptly against any attempt of stock exchange manipulations, false trading, market rigging, spreading false rumour, insider trading etc.

(b) Enforcement of control and regulatory mechanism
Mere existence of rules and regulation, however comprehensive it might be, are not sufficient to restore market efficiency if these are not seriously implemented. Though governing body of each stock exchange is mainly broker dominated, it must act impartially for the greater interest of the market and should not hesitate to enforce rules and regulations indiscriminately even if it hurts the interests of some of the members. Securities and Exchange Board of India (SEBI) must act as a watch dog and keep constant vigilance on the functioning of governing bodies.

(c) Improvement of accounting and reporting standard
Accounting and reporting standard must be improved in line with global standard. Audited corporate financial information that conforms to the standards of generally accepted accounting principles is essential. This is particularly important to satisfy the foreign investors.

(d) Prompt and efficient disclosure of price sensitive information

As required in the listing agreement, steps are to be taken to make it mandatory for prompt disclosure of price sensitive information failing which management of the company should be penalised. This will minimise rumour led speculative activities.

The above regulatory measures are particularly important when the country is eager to integrate its markets with the international financial system. Without effective regulation and enforcement, domestic and offsore investors will be reluctant to commit resources to Indian market. The government should, however, limit regulations to those needed to correct market failures that arise in unregulated markets and should not impede the development of the market. If the rules and regulations become stringent, they stifle private initiative and discourage companies from going public. The challenge is, therefore, to attain a balance between a system that ensures adequate protection for investors and one that does not deter market growth.

4. *On Restructuring of Interest Rate*

Number of committees, ignoring the roots, suggested numerous superficial measures to curb the role of outside finance in speculative activities of Indian stock market. The scam, however, revealed that the crux of the problem is the prevailing disproportionate rate of interest between artificially segmented "formal" and "informal" money market most suitable to arbitrage between them. There is a need to avert the anomalies in the return structure in financial markets so that outside financing can be arrested.

In fact a disparity in risk adjusted return exists among different segments of our financial system, that can only be minimised if the artificial barriers prevailing in the market are withered away. This integration will allow a coherent yield curve to emerge covering the entire financial system.

5. *On Role of Financial Institutions*

The government controlled financial institutions being "smart" money managers, are expected to follow the basic principle of investment theory-"buy low and sell high". Such policies in principle could smooth out transitory, noise trader induced fluctuation while allowing prices to adjust to persistent changes in fundamentals. This form of institutional participation raises the ratio of "smart" to "dumb" money in the market place by placing its enormous wealth on the smart, stabilizing side. Such action will increase the relative strength and thereby welfare of existing sophisticated investors and marginalize the influence of noise traders on the market (De Long et al., 1989). The view is also supported by empirical evidences which show that greater the institutional trading, the higher the efficiency of the market (Reilly and Wright, 1984).

Sophisticated investors in the private sector virtually lack adequate resources and nerve to successfully counteract irrational swings in demand that accompany boom and bust (Kindleberger, 1978).[12] Thus we propose the government controlled financial institutions, namely, Unit Trust and Life Insurance Corporation of India with their massive wealth would come forward to arbitrage and thereby to stabilize the market (see Friedman, 1953 and Fama, 1965), the role presumably they failed to perform in the last stock market tragedy.[13]

In order to increase the supply of equity shares, the financial institutions, the major shareholders of Indian corporate sector, should be allowed to unload their holdings in favour of individual shareholders by emerging gradually as net seller of equity. The approach is also consistent with their functions.

6. *On Short-term Capital Gains Tax*

In an extreme situation, when noise driven price movement can in no way be checked by other available measures, we would prefer short-term capital gains tax as high as it is required. The imposition of such tax would eliminate noise traders' incentive to speculate on their misperceptions and thus stabilize price at a constant fundamental level (De Long et al., 1989).

Capital gains tax can prevent illness, of course, at the cost of liquidity of the market. If there are few transactions, investors become locked in and for "immediacy reasons" developed by Grossman and Miller (1988) they might even stay out of the stock market that could result in the reduction of capital stock. If liquidity is socially valuable, such tax will do more harm than good. Hence, social welfare function should be taken cognizence while imposing it even for a shorter period (De Long et al., 1989).

All these above mentioned reforms in the capital market are necessary but not sufficient. Although the market started showing higher maturity and greater efficiency, there is still room for further improvement. The stock market in India is far away from full transparency and market discipline and has not yet been fully integrated with the rest of the countries of the world. There is a need for greater transparency and integration of the Indian stock market with the rest of the world, so that foreign capital can be attracted on a large and significant scale. For this, the rupee should be made fully convertible on capital account also. The convertibility of Indian Rupee on capital account will make the financial system in India more efficient and thereby will remove the major defects of the capital market. Finally, the authorities concerned should keep constant touch with the changing financial scenario around the world and accordingly appropriate measures should be taken to make the market well equipped at par international standard.

NOTES

1. Economists however favour to divide the development process of Indian economy into three phases: phase of self-reliance or the early stage of planning (1950–65), phase of systematic crisis emerging from mixed economy (1965 to late 70s), phase of economic liberalisation to overcome the emerging crisis (early 80s, and onward) (see Swamy Dalip, 1994).
2. See Chapter III and also Roy and Karmakar (1995).
3. See Chapter IV and also Roy and Karmakar (1994).
4. See Keynes J.M. (1964), Singh, A. (1993), and Ilene Grabel (1995).
5. In the main study, we have measured volatility for a period spanning over 1935 to 1992. The present measure (Table 5.2) includes three more years i.e., 1993, 1994 & 1995 to show the volatility of pre and post liberalisation periods. The data series for the additional three years has been collected from the same index number of share prices, i.e., "The Economic Times Index Number of Ordinary Share Prices", compiled and published by the Economic Times on daily basis.
6. It is a perennial problem of Indian stock market. Number of committees including Patel Committee unveiled the menace of outside financing in the speculative transactions of our stock market.
7. Noisy price, in fact, ensued massive participation of "naive-trend chasing" investors that further increased the magnitude of noise in price.

8. Share trading velocity measures the number of times the issued share capital of a company (or a group of companies) is turned over in the market during a year. It is derived as follows:

$$\frac{\text{Total trading volume in the shares during a year}}{\text{Market capitalisation (i.e., market value of all shares of the company/companies)}}$$

9. Insider trading generally means trading in the shares of a company by the persons who are in the management of the company or are close to them on the basis of undisclosed price sensitive information regarding the working of the company, which they possess but not available to others. Such trading as it involves misuse of confidential information is unethical, tantamounting to betrayal of fiduciary position of trust and confidence.
10. At present as much as 90% of the volume of trading in the Stock Exchange is of a speculative character.
11. For a discussion on different issues on privatization in the global context, see Lieberman, Ira W (1993).
12. This argument is related to the ideas of Grossman and Miller (1988) on market liquidity, although the authors do not discuss a potential role for the government controlled financial institutions.
13. Financial Institutions were, in fact, sandwitched between the conflicting role they played traditionally as guardians of the market and the new role to perform-in financial terms conferred upon them by the New Economic Policy. Finally, they preferred to fish in the troubled water in their quest to provide short term benefits to its unit-holders and suffered a severe setback alike other naive traders when the bubble burst.

REFERENCES

Cho, Y.J. "Inefficiencies from Financial Liberalisation in the Absence of Well-Functioning Equity markets", *Journal of Money, Credit and Banking*, Vol. 18, No. 2 (May 1986), pp. 191–99.

Cochrane, J.H. "Volatility Tests and Efficient Markets", A Review Essay, *Journal of Monetary Economics*, 27 (1991), pp. 463–485.

Dailami, Mansoor and Michael Atkin, 1990. "Stock Markets in Developing Countries: Key Issues and a Research Agenda, Policy Research Working Paper 515, World Bank, Country Economics Department, Washington, D.C.

De Long, J. Bradford; Andrei Shleifer; Lawrence H. Summers; and Robert J. Waldman. "The Size and Incidence of the Losses from Noise Trading", *Journal of Finance*, Vol. XLIV, No. 3 (July 1989), pp. 681–696.

Edwards, F.R. "Does Futures Trading Increase Stock Market Volatility?" *Financial Analysts Journal*, Jan.–Feb., 1988, pp. 63–69.

Fama, Eugene F. "The Behaviour of Stock Market Prices", *Journal of Business*, 38 (Jan. 1965), pp. 34–105.

Figlewski, Stephen. "Market Efficiency in a Market with Heterogeneous Information", *Journal of Political Economy*, Vol. 86, No. 4 (1978), pp. 581–97.

Friedman, Milton. "The Case for Flexible Exchange Rates" in M. Friedman, *"Essays in Positive Economics"* (1953), Chicago: University of Chicago Press.

Grossman, Sanford and Merton Miller. "Liquidity and Market Structure", *Journal of Finance,* 43 (1988), pp. 617–633.

Ilene Grabel, "Assessing the Impact of Financial Liberalisation on Stock Market Volatility in Selected Developing Countries", *Journal of Development Studies,* Vol. 31, No. 6, Aug. 1995, pp. 903–17.

Keynes, J.M. *"The General Theory of Employment, Interest and Money"*, New York, 1936.

Keynes, J.M. (1931). "An Economic analysis of Unemployment", *in Collected Writings,* Vol. XIII (MacMillan, London, 1973).

Kindleberger, Charles P. "Manias, Panic, and Crashes", 1978, (Basic Books, New York).

Lieberman, Ira W. "Privatisation: The Theme of the 1990s, An Overview", *Columbia Journal of World Business* (Spring 1993), pp. 7–17.

McKinnon, Ronald. *"Money and Capital in Economic Development"*, Washington, D.C.: The Brookings Institution (1973).

Reilly, Frank K. and David J. Wright. "Block Trading and Aggregate Stock Price Volatility", *Financial Analysts Journal* (March–April 1984), pp. 54–60.

Roy, M. and Karmakar, M. "Irrational Movement of Share Prices: Evidences and Implications", *Journal of Indian School of Political Economy,* (July–September 1994), pp.673–83.

Roy, M. and Karmakar, M. "Stock Market Volatility: Roots and Results", Vikalpa, Vol. 20, No. 1 (Jan.–March 1995), pp. 37–48.

Shaw, Edward (1973). *"Financial Deepening in Economic Development"*, New York; Oxford University Press.

Shleifer, Andrei and Lawrence H. Summers. "The Noise Trader Approach to Finance", *Journal of Economic Perspectives,* Vol. 4, No. 2 (Spring 1990), pp. 19–33.

Singh, A. "Should Developing Countries Encourage Stock Markets?" *United Nations Conference on Trade and Development Review,* 1993, pp. 11–12.

Swamy, Dalip S. *"The Political Economy of Industralisation"*, Sage India, 1994.

APPENDIX A

A BRIEF DESCRIPTION OF SOME HISTORICAL BUBBLES INCLUDING RECENT EXPERIENCES

- TULIP MANIA OF 17TH CENTURY HOLLAND
  In the late 1500s and early 1600s, the Dutch paid exorbitant amounts for tulips. This craze spread to England, where speculators lost fortunes on a single tulip bulb when the fad ceased.
- MISSISSIPPI SCHEME
  Law (1968) devised a scheme to generate private prosperity and state income in France through colonial and commercial exploitation of French Louisiana. When the French government chartered (1717) Law's company of the West, share prices soared from 500 to 18000 livres. From 1719 to 1720, the company absorbed all other French trading companies, the state's tax collection, coinage and debt, and Law's national bank. When expected profits did not materialize, panic selling burst the bubble in October 1720. This fiasco bred great public distrust of state banking.
- SOUTH SEA BUBBLE
  The South Sea Company was founded in 1711 by Harley, Earl of Oxford, for world trade. In seven short years, investors were reaping 100 per cent in interest. In 1720, the company proposed that it take over the national debt, and parliament accepted. The stock price rose from 128.5 points in eight months. Robert Walpole was able to restore the company's credit and save the Whig government despite the fact that when the bubble burst many banks failed and investors were ruined.

- BASEBALL CARD MANIA OF 20th CENTURY AMERICA
  Baseball picture cards with a signature sell for thousands of dollars, and price is based on condition of the card, much like tulip mania when the tulip condition was analysed.
- USA BEAR MARKET OF 1973–1974
  The USA market lost approximately 50 per cent of its value.
- BIOTECH-STOCK CRAZE OF THE 1980s
  Investors ignored value parameters on earnings and were buying issues strictly on the basis of popularity.
- WORLD MARKET CRASH IN OCTOBER 1987
  All major world stock markets declined substantially in October 1987-an exceptional occurrence. On October 19, 1987, the Dow Jones Industrial Average (DJIA) fell from 2246.7 to 1738.4, over 508 points. This was the largest one day of absolute as well as percentage (about 22.5%) drop since the DJIA began computing index number in 1885. Of course, the US market was not the first to decline sharply. Non-Japanese Asian markets began a severe decline on October 19 (their time). The decline was echoed first by a number of European markets, then by North America and, finally, by Japan (Roll, Richard 1988).
- BUBBLE BURST IN JAPANESE ECONOMY 1990–92
  Stock prices and land prices in Japan increased at a very rapid pace in the late 1980s. The Nikkei 225 index of stock prices went from 9500 in December 1983 to 18700 in December 1986, and then to 38000 in 1989, more than doubling every three years. Average land prices in Tokyo doubled between the end of 1986 and the end of 1988. Stock prices peaked at the end of 1989, and land prices peaked around 1990–91. Once a turning point was reached, asset prices plummeted. (International Capital Markets: Developments, Prospects and Policy Issues, IMF, Aug. 1995).

APPENDIX B

1. *Close-to-close Standard Deviation Method*

The most commonly used measure of stock return volatility is standard deviation based on close-to-close price data (Jones and Wilson, 1989; Schwert, G.W., 1990; Cho and Frees, 1988).

Let $(P_1, P_2, \ldots, P_{n+1})$ be a set of share prices quoted at the close of each trading day. Then the standard deviaton of rate of return (r) on the share price, is traditionally estimated as follows: Letting $r_t = I_n (P_t/P_{t-1})$, $t = 1, 2, \ldots n$ = rate of return over the daily closing prices, then

$$\sigma = \left[\frac{1}{n}\sum_{t=1}^{n}(r_t - \bar{r})^2\right]^{1/2}$$

2. *Classical Estimator*

The classical estimation procedure employs

$$\hat{\sigma}_0^2 = (C_1 - C_0)^2,$$

as an unbiased estimator of σ^2 (variance of price changes). This very method is based on close-to-close price data. The advantage of the method is its simplicity and its freedom from obvious sources or error or bias. Its principal disadvantage is the fact that it ignores other readily available information which may contribute to estimator efficiency (Garman and Klass, 1980).

3. *Extreme Value Method*

Market volatility can also be examined by using alternative estimators of volatility, in addition to the standard close-to-close daily price changes. As it is alleged that much of the recent volatility has been in intraday price movements, rather than in day-to-day price changes (Edwards, Franklin R., 1988), intuition would tell us that high/low prices contain more information regarding volatility than do close-to-close prices. This intuition is correct. Parkinson had shown that simply using the daily high and low prices, the variance estimator

$$\hat{\sigma}_2^2 = [I_n(H_t) - I_n(D_t)]^2 / 4 I_n^2,$$

had an efficiency of 5.2 (Parkinson, M.D., 1980). Thus the use of these extreme values (the high and low prices) provides a far superior estimate to the traditional close-to-close variance.

4. *The Garman-Klass Estimator*

Garman and Klass (1980) while developing the idea originally introduced by Parkinson (1980) argue that improved volatility measures can be obtained by taking into account the daily high, low, and opening prices in addition to the traditionally used closing prices (Garman and Klass, 1980). The more 'practical' estimator proposed by them is a weighted average of Parkinson's high-low estimator ($\hat{\sigma}_2^2$) and the traditional close-to-close estimator ($\hat{\sigma}_0^2$) and is given by

$$\hat{\sigma}_5^2 = .5(H_t - D_t)^2 - .39(C_t - C_{t-1})^2$$

which has a greater efficiency $[\mathrm{Eff}(\hat{\sigma}_5^2) = 7.4]$, than that of Parkinson High-low estimator, and thus contains much more information of daily price movements.

Beckers (1983) empirically compared the two components $\hat{\sigma}_0^2$ and $\hat{\sigma}_2^2$ used in the weighted estimator $\hat{\sigma}_5^2$ by Garman and Klass (1980), and concluded that the Parkinson's estimator may contain information which is not reflected in the close-to-close variance (Beckers, S., 1983). Thus the daily price range provides a better indication of stock price volatility hence, may be considered as a more accurate estimator. The information content of the high-low data however varies across shares. Its empirical value increases significantly when these cross sectional differences are incorporated in a new variance estimator adjusted as follows:

5. *'Adjusted' High-Low Estimator*

Beckers proposes the new adjusted estimator $\hat{\sigma}_{6,n,t} = \hat{a}_{n,t} + \hat{b}_{n,t}\, \hat{\sigma}_{2,n,t}$ which appears to be more "accurate" than the traditional close-to-close measure. In fact in the pairwise comparison Garman-Klass estimator $\hat{\sigma}_5^2$ was consistently out performed by $\hat{\sigma}_6$ (Beckers, S., 1983).

6. *A New Estimation Method*

Since publication of Parkinson's high-low estimator, a number of researchers in their pursuit to sharpen the said model suggested numerous techniques and the last inclusion in this queue is Kunitomo (1992). Model suggested is—

$$\hat{\sigma}^2(k) = \frac{1}{nT}\left(\frac{6}{n^2}\right)\sum_{i=1}^{n} R_i^2$$

based on the adjusted range $R_i = \underset{t \in I_i}{\mathrm{Max}}(Y_t) - \underset{t \in I_t}{\min}(Y_t)$

where Y(t) is transformed from X(t) used by parkinson to find the range (Kunitomo, N., 1992). The efficiency of his estimator $\hat{\sigma}^2(k)$ is about 10 in comparison with the standard sample variance estimator

$$\left[\hat{\sigma}^2(c) = \frac{1}{T(n-1)}\sum_{i=1}^{n}(d_i - \bar{d})^2\right]$$

Since the efficiency of the Parkinson's estimator is about 4.91, Kunitomo's estimation method may considerably improve the estimation methods, already known in financial economics.

APPENDIX C

TOP 20 COMPANIES BY TURNOVER (1988–1989)

1. ACC
2. Bajaj Auto
3. Bombay Dyeing
4. Century Text
5. Enka
6. Colgate
7. Eskayef
8. Grasim Industries
9. Indian Rayon
10. J.K. Synthetics
11. L & T
12. Mahindra & Mahindra
13. Orkay Mills
14. Premier Auto
15. Reliance Industry
16. Southern Petro
17. SKF Bearing
18. Telco
19. Tata Steel
20. Tata Tea

Source: Bombay Stock Exchange Official Directory

APPENDIX D

THE LIST OF 30 SHARES INITIALLY USED FOR P_t AND D_t SERIES.

1. Titaghur Paper Mills
2. Polychem Ltd.
3. Surat Electricity
4. Sutlej Cotton Mills
5. Tata Hydro Electric Power Supply
6. Tata Power Co. Ltd.
7. Tata Iron and Steel Co. Ltd.
8. Kesoram Industries & Cotton Mills
9. Metur Chemicals & Industries Corproation
10. Supreme Industries Ltd.
11. Aluminium Corporation of India
12. Hindustan Gas & Industries Ltd.
13. Indian Dyestuff Industries Ltd.
14. Amalgamated Electricity Co. Ltd.
15. Ahmedabad Electricity Co. Ltd.
16. Andhra Valley Power Supply Co.
17. Bombay Suburban Electricity
18. Bajaj Electronic Ltd.
19. Asian Electronic Ltd.
20. India Cement
21. Kemp & Co. Ltd.
22. Sayaji Mills Ltd.
23. United Breweries
24. Indian Rubber Regenerating
25. Ruby Mills
26. Western India Plywood Ltd.
27. Cellulose Product of India Ltd.
28. Indian Cable
29. Universal Cable
30. Sirdar Carbonic Gas Ltd.

APPENDIX E

Table 1. Market Capitalization of Asia/Pacific Equity Markets, Excluding Japan (US $ Billions)

Country	1982	Jan 1994	% GDP (1994)
China	NA	45.4	0.2
Hong Kong	21.6	375.0	298.0
India	0.1	34.1	54.0
Indonesia	0.1	34.1	21.0
Malaysia	13.9	194.0	285.0
Pakistan	1.9	12.0	24.0
The Philippines	2.0	37.0	64.0
Singapore	11.7	140.0	226.0
South Korea	4.4	155.4	44.0
Sri Lanka	NA	3.0	39.0
Taiwan	5.1	197.0	85.0
Thailand	1.3	118.0	88.0

Table 2. Number and Size of Companies Listed

Country	1982	1993	Average size 1993 (US $ Millions)
China	NA	246	189
Hong Kong	210	285	773
India (Bombay in parenthesis)	2400	7000 (3000)	21 (44 bn)
Indonesia	16	160	213
Malaysia	260	425	746
Pakistan	NA	652	18.4
The Philippines	200	180	206
Singapore	112	200	700
South Korea	334	710	218
Sri Lanka	NA	200	15
Taiwan	115	290	679
Thailand	80	375	317

Source: Clemente, Lilia, "Investing in Asia's Emerging Equity Market", *The Columbia Journal of World Business*, Summer 1994, p. 96.

APPENDIX F

Volatility in Selected Equity Markets, 1983–92[a]

Country	1982–92	1983–88	1989–92
Developing Countries			
Hong Kong	8.1	10.0	6.8
India	10.0	7.5	12.8
Korea	8.2	7.5	9.0
Pakistan	6.7	2.8	8.8
Thailand	7.7	7.1	8.7
Developed Countries			
Japan	4.7	3.3	5.9
United Kingdom	4.4	4.7	4.1
United States	3.4	3.7	3.0

[a]Measured by the standard deviation of the percentage change in equity prices (at the end month) in domestic country. Volatility in developing markets is higher than that in developed countries.

Source: EL-ERIAN and KUMAR, "Emgering Equity Markets in Middle Eastern Countries", *IMF Staff Papers*, Vol. 42, No. 2 (Jan. 1995), p. 328.

APPENDIX G

Comparative Analysis of Share Trading Volume & Share Trading Velocity of Certain Groups of Shares of BSE, 1989–90 and New York Exchanges, 1989

Groups of Shares		Percentage of trading volume		Trading Velocity	
		BSE	NYSE	BSE	NYSE
Top 5 by trading volume					
BSE	NYSE				
Tata Steel	ATT	13.8	0.93	1.41	0.36
ACC	IBM	9.6	0.81	12.30	0.58
Tata Engineering	Texaco	7.0	0.73	0.91	1.11
Reliance Industries	Gen. Electronics	6.8	0.73	1.94	0.33
Bombay Dyeing	Exxon	3.7	0.65	4.68	0.15
Sub Total of top 5		40.9	3.9	1.81	0.34
Top 50 by trading volume		82.1	21.00	NA	1.04
Shares other than top 50 by trading volume		17.9	79.00	NA	0.19
All Shares		100.0	100.0	0.52	0.57

Source: Gupta L.C. "Stock Exchange Trading in India—Agenda for Reform" (1992), pp. 7, 9.

APPENDIX H

Frequency Distribution of BSE-listed Companies by percentage of Days Traded during April 1988–March 1989

Sl. No.	Percentage of Trading Days	No. of Companies	Percentage to Column Total
1.	More than 90% of days	456	20.0
2.	More than 80% and upto 90%	152	6.7
3.	More than 70% and upto 80%	94	4.1
4.	More than 60% and upto 70%	57	2.5
5.	More than 50% and upto 60%	72	3.2
	Sub total (1–5)	831	36.5
6.	More than 40% and upto 50%	66	2.9
7.	More than 30% and upto 40%	51	2.2
8.	More than 20% and upto 30%	79	3.5
9.	More than 10% and upto 20%	93	4.1
10.	Upto 10%	1155	50.8
	Sub total (6–10)	1444	63.5
	Grand Total	2275	100.0

Source: Paul Joseph, "An Investigation into the causes for thinly-traded shares in the stock exchanges in India, and alternative sources of capital for companies", (MBA thesis submitted to University of Hull, UK, in 1990, p. 36, unpublished). Also reproduced in L.C. Gupta, "Stock Exchange Trading in India—Agenda for Reform", 1992, p. 56.

SELECT BIBLIOGRAPHY

BOOKS

Andreassen, Paul and Stephen Kraus. Judgemental Prediction by Extrapolation, Harvard University, Mimeo, 1988.

Box, G.E.P. and G.M. Jenkins. Time Series Analysis for Forecasting and Control, San Francisco: Holden-Day, 1970.

Cootner, Paul (ed.). The Random Character of Stock Market Prices, Cambridge: M.I,T., 1964.

Cox, J.C. and Rubinstein, M. Option Market, Englewood Cliffs, N.J.: Prentice Hall, 1985.

Dixit, R.K. Behaviour of Share Prices and Investment in India, Deep & Deep Publications, New Delhi, 1986.

Dreman, Devid N. Psychology and the Stock Market, *AMACOM*, 135 West 50th Street, New York, N.Y. 10020 (1977).

Eatwell, J., Milgate, M. and Newman, P. "The New Palgrave: A Dictionary of Economics", London: MacMillan, 1987, (eds.).

Friedman, Milton. Essays in Positive Economics, Chicago, University Chicago Press, 1953.

Gadgil, D.R. The Industrial Evolution of India, Oxford University Press, Madras, 1929.

Galbraith, John K. The Great Crash, (Boston: Houghton Mifflin Co., 1961).

Goldsmith, Raymond W. The Financial Development of India, 1860–1977, Oxford University Press, Delhi, 1983.

Gupta, L.C. "Stock Exchange Trading in India—Agenda for Reform" (1992).

Gupta, O.P. Behaviour of Share Prices in India: A Test of Market Efficiency, National Publishing House, New Delhi, 1985.

Gupta, Umrao L. Working of Stock Exchanges in India, Thomson Press (India) Limited, New Delhi, 1972.

Keynes, J.M. The General Theory of Employment, Interest and Money, London: MacMillan, 1936.

Keynes, John M. (1931), An Economic Analysis of Unemployment, in *Collected Writings*, Vol. XIII MacMillan, London, 1973.

Kindleberger, Charles P. Manias, Panic and Crashes, 1978, Basic Books, New York.

McKinnon, Ronald. "Money and Capital in Economic Development", Washington, DC: The Brookings Institution, 1973.

Shaw Edward. "Financial Deepening in Economic Development", New York: Oxford University Press, 1973.

Shiller, Robert J. Market Volatility, The MIT Press, Cambridge, 1989.

Soros, George. The Alchemy of Finance, Simon and Schuster, New York, 1987.

Swamy, Dalip S. "The Political Economy of Industrialisation", Sage India, 1994.

ARTICLES

Admati, Anat R. "The Informational Role of Prices", *Journal of Monetary Economics*, Vol. 28, (1991), pp. 347–361.

Amihud, Yakov and Haim Mendelson. "Volatility, Efficiency, and Trading: Evidence from the Japanese Stock Market", *Journal of Finance*, Vol. XLVI No. 5 (December 1991). pp. 1765–1789.

Amihud, Yakov, Haim Mendelson, and Maurizio Murgia. "Stock Market Microstructure and Return Volatility", *Journal of Banking and Finance*, Vol. 14, (1990), pp. 423–40.

Arbel, Avner and Bikki Jaggi. "Market Information Assimination Related to Extreme Daily Price Jumps", *Financial Analysts Journal* (November–December 1982), pp. 60–66.

Bachelier, Louis. "Theorie de la Speculation" (Paris: Gauthier-Villars, 1900), and reprinted in English in Cootner (ed.), 1964.

Ball, Ray and Phillip Brown. "An Empirical Evaluation of Accounting Income Number", *Journal of Accounting Research*, 6 (Autumn, 1968), pp. 159–78.

Barua, Samir K. and Jayanth R. Varma. "Securities Scam: Genesis, Mechanics, and Impact", *Vikalpa*, Vol. 18, No. 1 (January–March 1993), pp.3–12.

Baumol, William J. "Speculation, Profitability and Stability", *Review of Economics and Statistics*, 39 (August 1957), pp. 263–71.

Beckers, S. "Standard Deviations Implied in Option Prices as Predicators of Future Stock Price Variability", *Journal of Banking and Finance*, 5 (September 1981), pp. 363–82.

Beckers, S. "Variances of Security Prices Returns Based on High, Low and Closing Prices", *Journal of Business*, Vol. 56, No. 1, (1983), pp. 97–112.

Black, Fisher. "Noise", *Journal of Finance*, Vol. XLI, No. 3 (July 1986), pp. 529–543.

Blanchard, O. and M. Watson. "Bubbles, Rational Expectations and Financial Markets", in Crises in the Economic and Financial Structure, ed. by P. Watchtel. Lexington Mass: Lexington Books, 1982.

Boldt, Bob L. and Hall L. Arbit. "Efficient Markets and the Professional Investor", *Financial Analysts Journal* (July–August 1984), pp. 22–23.

Butler, Kirt C. and S.J. Malaikah. "Efficiency and Inefficiency in Thinly Traded Stock Markets: Kuwait and Saudi Arabia", *Journal of Banking and Finance*, Vol. 16, (1992), pp. 197–210

Case, Karl E. and Robert J. Shiller. "The Behaviour of Home Buyers in Boom and Post-Boom Market", *New England Economic Review* (Nov./Dec. 1988), pp. 29–45.

Cass, D. and Shell, K. "Do Sunspots Matter?", *Journal of Political Economy,* (1983), Vol. 91, No. 2.

Cho, D. Chinhyung and Edward W. Frees. "Estimating the Volatility of Discrete Stock Prices", *Journal of Finance,* Vol. XLIII, No. 2 (June 1988), pp. 451–65.

Cho, Y.J. "Inefficiencies from Financial Liberalisation in the Absence of Well-functioning Equity Markets", *Journal of Money, Credit and Banking,* Vol. 18, No. 2 (May 1986), pp. 191–99.

Cochrane, John H. "Volatility Tests and Efficient Markets", A Review Essay, *Journal of Monetary Economics,* 27, (1991) pp. 463–485.

Cootner, P. "Stock Prices: Random vs. Systematic Changes", *Industrial Management Review,* 3 (Spring 1962), pp. 24–45.

Clemente, Lilia. "Investing in Asia's Emerging Equity Market", *The Columbia Journal of World Business,* (Summer 1994), p. 96.

Cutler, David M., James, M. Poterba, and Lawrence H. Summers, "What Moves Stock Prices?", *The Journal of Portfolio Management,* (Spring 1989), No. 15, pp. 4–12.

Dailami, Mansoor and Michael Atkin, "Stock Markets in Developing Countries: Key Issues and a Research Agenda, Policy Research Working Paper 515, World Bank, Country Economics Department, Washingon, D.C., (1990).

De Long, J. Bradford, Andrei Shleifer, Lawrence H. Summers, and Robert J. Waldmann. "The Size and Incidence of the Losses from Noise Trading", *Journal of Finance,* Vol. XLIV, No. 3 (July 1989), pp. 681–696.

De Long, J. Bradford, Andrei Shleifer, Lawrence H. Summers, and Robert J. Waldman. "Positive Feedback Investment Strategies and Destabilizing Rational Speculation", *Journal of Finance,* Vol. XLV, No. 2 (June 1990). pp. 379–395.

De Long, J. Bradford, Andrei Shleifer, Lawrence H. Summers and Robert J. Waldman. "Noise Trader Risk in Financial Markets", *Journal of Political Economy,* Vol. 98, No. 4 (1990), pp. 703–737.

De Long, J. Bradford, Andrei Shleifer, Lawrence H. Summers, and Robert J. Waldman. "The Survival of Noise Traders in Financial Markets", *Journal of Business,* Vol. 64, No. 1, (1991), pp. 1–19.

Dimon, Elroy and Paul Marsh. "Volatility Forecasting without Data-Snopping", *Journal of Banking and Finance,* 14, (1990), pp. 399–421.

Edwards, Franklin R. "Does Futures Trading Increase Stock Market Volatility?" *Financial Analysts Journal* (January–February 1988), pp. 63–69.

El-Erian and Kumar, 'Emerging Equity Markets in Middle Eastern Countries", *IMF Staff Papers,* Vol. 42, No. 2 (June 1995), p. 328

Errunza, Vihang R. "Emerging Markets: A New Opportunity for Improving Global Portfolio Performance", *Financial Analysts Journal* (September–October 1983), p. 51–58.

Fama, Eugene F. "The Behavior of Stock Market Prices", *Journal of Business,* 38 (January 1965), pp. 34–105.

Fama, Eugene F. "Efficient Capital Market: A Review of Theory and Empirical Work", *Journal of Finance* (May 1970), pp. 383–417.

Fama, Eugene F. "Efficient Capital Markets: II", *Journal of Finance*, Vol. XLVI, No. 5 (December 1991), pp. 1575–1617.

Fama, Eugene F. and Kenneth R. French. "Permanent and Temporary Components of Stock Prices", *Journal of Political Economy*, Vol. 96, No. 2, (1988), pp. 246–73.

Fama, Eugene F. and Marshall Blume. "Filter Rules and Stock Market Trading Profits", *Journal of Business*, 39 (Special Supplement, January 1966), pp. 226–41.

Fama, Eugene F, L. Fisher, M. Jensen and R. Roll. "The Adjustment of Stock Prices to New Information", *International Economic Review* (February 1969), pp. 1–21.

Farrell, Michael J. "Profitable Speculation", *Economica*, 33 (May 1966), pp. 183–193.

Ferguson, Robert, "On Crashes", *Financial Analysts Journal* (March–April 1989), pp. 42–52.

Figlewski, Stephen. "Market Efficiency in a Market with Heterogeneous Information", *Journal of Political Economy*, Vol. 86, No. 4 (1978), pp. 581–97.

Figlewski, Stephen. "Subjective Information and Market Efficiency in a Betting Market", *Journal of Political Economy*, 87 (February 1979), pp. 75–88.

Flavin, Marjorie A. "Excess Volatility in the Financial Markets: A Reassessment of the Empirical Evidence", *Journal of Political Economy*, Vol. 91 (December 1983), pp. 929–95.

Garber, Peter M. "Famous First Bubbles", *Journal of Economic Perspectives*, Vol. 4, No. 2 (Spring 1990), pp. 35–54.

Garman, M. and M. Klass. "On the Estimation of Security Price Volatilities from Historical Data", *Journal of Business*, Vol. 3, No. 1, (1980), pp. 67–78.

Gennotte, Gerard and Hayne Leland. "Market Liquidity, Hedging, and Crashes", *The American Economic Review*, Vol. 80, No. 5 (December 1990), pp. 999–1021.

Greenwald, Bruce and Jeremy Stein. "The Task Force Report: The Reasoning behind the Recommendations", *Journal of Economic Perspectives*, Vol. 2, No. 3 (Summer 1988), pp. 3–23.

Grossman, Sanford J. "On the Efficiency of Competitive Stock Markets Where Traders Have Diverse Information", *Journal of Finance*, 31 (May 1976), pp. 573–58.

Grossman, Sanford J. "The Existence of Futures Markets, Noisy Rational Expectations and Informational Externalities", *Review of Economic Studies*, 44(3), (September 1977), pp. 431–449.

Grossman, Sanford J. "Further Results on Informational Efficiency of Competitive Stock Markets", *Journal of Economic Theory*, 18 (June 1978), pp. 81–101.

Grossman, Sanford J. "Program Trading and Market Volatility: A Report on Interday Relationships", *Financial Analysts Journal* (July–August 1988), pp. 18 20.

Grossman, Sanford J. and Joseph E. Stiglitz. "Information and Competitive Price System", *American Economic Review*, 66 (May 1976), pp. 246 53.

Grossman, Sanford J. and Joseph E. Stiglitz. "On the Impossibility of Informationally Efficient Market", *American Economic Review*, 70 (June 1980), pp. 393–408.

Grossman, Sanford J. and Merton Miller. "Liquidity and Market Structure", *Journal of Finance*, 43, (1988), pp. 617–633.

Grossman, Sanford J. and Robert J. Shiller. "The Determinants of the Variability of Stock Market Prices". *American Economic Review*, Vol. 71, No. 2 (May 1981), pp. 222–227.

Grubel, Herbert G. "The Peter Principle and the Efficient Market Hypothesis", *Financial Analysts Journal* (November–December 1979) pp. 72–75.

Harris, L. "S & P 500 Cash Stock Price Volatilities", *Journal of Finance*, Vol. XLIV, No. 5, (Dec. 1989), pp. 1155–1175.

Hart, Oliver D. and David M. Kreps. "Price Destabilizing Speculation", *Journal of Political Economy*, Vol. 94, No. 5, (1986), pp. 927–952.

Ilene Grabel. "Assessing the Impact of Financial Liberalisation on Stock Market Volatility in Selected Developing Countries", *Journal of Development Studies*, Vol. 31, No. 6, (August 1995), pp. 903–917.

Jaffe, Jeffrey J. and Robert L. Winkler. "Optimum Speculation Against on Efficient Market", *Journal of Finance*, Vol. XXXI, No. 1 (March 1976), pp. 49–61.

Jensen, Michael C. "Some Anomalous Evidence Regarding Market Efficiency", *Journal of Financial Economics*, 6 (June–September 1978), pp. 95–102.

Jones, P. and W. Wilson. "Is Stock Price Volatility Increasing?", *Financial Analysts Journal* (November–December 1989), pp. 20–26.

Kawaller, Ira G., Paul D. Koch and Timothy W. Koch. "Intraday Relationships Between Volatility in S & P 500 Futures Prices and Volatility in the S & P 500 Index", *Journal of Banking and Finance*, Vol. 14, (1990), pp. 373–97.

Keane, Simon M. "October `87 and the Efficient Market", Editorial Viewpoint, *Financial Analysts Journal* (January–February 1988), pp. 6–7.

Kemp, A.G. and G.C. Reid. "The Random Walk Hypothesis and the Rcent Behaviour of Equity Prices in Britain", *Economica*, Vol. 38 (1971), pp. 28–51

Kendall, M.G. "The Analysis of Economic Time Series—Part I Prices", *Journal of the Royal Statistical Society*, Series A (General), Vol. 116, pt. 1, (1953), pp. 11–25.

Keynes, J.M. (1931) "An Economic analysis of Unemployment", in *Collected Writings*, Vol. XIII (MacMillan, London, 1973).

Kleidon, Allan W. "Variance Bounds Tests and Stock Price Valuation Models", *Journal of Political Economy*, 94 (October 1986), pp. 953–1001.

Kleidon, Allan W. "The Probability of Gross Violations of a Present Value Variance Inequality: Reply", *Journal of Political Economy*, Vol. 96, No. 5, (1988), pp. 1093–1096.

Kritzman, Mark. "What Practitioners Need to Know . . . About Estimating Volatility", *Financial Analysts Journal* (July–August 1991), pp. 22–25.

Kunitomo, N. "Improving the Parkinson Method of Estimating Security Price Volatilities", *Journal of Business*, Vol. 65, No. 2 (1992), pp. 295–302.

Kyle, A.S. "Continuous Auctions and Insider Trading", *Econometrica*, 47 (1985), pp. 1315–1336.

Latham, Mark, "Informational Efficiency and Information Subsets", *Journal of Finance,* Vol. XLI, No. 1 (March 1986), pp. 39–52.

LeBaron, Blake. "Some Relations between Volatility and Serial Correlations in Stock Market Returns", *Journal of Business,* Vol. 65, No. 2 (1992), pp. 199–219.

Leland, Hayne and Mark Rubinstein. "Comments on the Market Crash: Six Months After", *Journal of Economic Perspectives,* Vol. 2 No. 3 (Summer 1988), pp. 45–50.

LeRoy Stephen F. "Efficiency and the Variability of Asset Prices", *American Economic Review,* Vol. 74, No. 4 (May 1984), pp. 183–87.

LeRoy Stephen F. and Porter, Richard D. "The Present Value Relation: Test Based on Implied Variance Bounds", *Econometrica,* 49 (May 1981), pp. 555–74.

Lieberman, Ira W. "Privatisation: The Theme of the 1990s, An Overview", *Columbia Journal of World Business* (Spring 1993), pp. 9–17.

Lintner, John. "Security Prices, Risk, and Maximum Gains From Diversification", *Journal of Finance,* 20 (December 1965), pp. 587–615.

Mandelbrot, B. "The Variation of Certain Speculative Prices", *Journal of Business,* 36 (October 1963), pp. 394–419.

Mandelbrot, B. "Forecasts of Future Prices, Unbiased Markets, and Martingale Models", *Journal of Business* (January 1966), pp. 242–255.

Mankiw, N. Gregory, David Romer and Mathew D. Shapiro. "An Unbiased Reexamination of Stock Market Volatility", *Journal of Finance,* Vol. XL, No. 3 (July 1985), pp. 677–87.

Marsh, A. and Robert C. Merton. "Dividend Variability and Variance Bounds Tests for the Rationality of Stock Market Prices", Working Paper 1584–84 (Massachusetts Institute of Technology, Alfred P. Sloan School of Management, August 1984).

McConnel, Walter S. and Stephen D. Leit. "Inflation, Stock Prices and Job Creation", *Financial Analysts Journal* (March–April, 1977), pp. 25–29.

Meese, Richard. "Testing for Bubbles in Exchange Markets: A Case of Sparking Rates?" *Journal of Political Economy* 94 (April 1986), pp. 345–73.

Neiderhoffer, V. and M.F.M. Osborne. "Market Making and Reversal on the Stock Exchange", *Journal of the American Statistical Association,* 61 (December 1966), pp. 897–916.

Osborne, M.F.M. "Periodic Structure in the Brownian Motion of Stock Prices", *Operations Research,* 10 (May–June 1962), pp. 345–79.

Parkinson, M. "The Extreme Value Method for Estimating the Variance of the Rate of Return", *Journal of Business,* Vol. 53, No. 1, (1980), pp. 61–65.

Poon, Ser-Huang and Stephen J. Taylor. "Stock Returns and Volatility: An Empirical Study of the UK Stock Market", *Journal of Banking and Finance,* Vol. 16, (1992), pp. 37–59.

Poterba, James M. and Lawrence H. Summers. "The Persistence of Volatility and Stock Market Fluctuations", *American Economic Review,* Vol. 76, No. 5 (December 1986), pp. 1142–1151.

Reilly, Frank K. and David J. Wright. "Block Trading and Aggregate Stock Price Volatility", *Financial Analyst Journal* (March–April 1984), pp. 54–60.

Roll, Richard. "The International Crash of October 1987", *Financial Analysts Journal* (September–October 1988) pp. 19–35.

Ross, Stephen A. "Information and Volatility: The No-Arbitrage Martingale Approach to Timing and Resolution Irrelevency", *Journal of Finance*, Vol. XLIV, No. 1 (March 1989), pp. 1–17.

Roy, M. and M. Karmakar, "Irrational Movement of Share Price: Evidences and Implications", *Journal of Indian School of Political Economy*, (July–September 1994), pp. 673–683.

Roy, M. and M. Karmakar, "Stock Market Volatility: Roots and Resuts", *Vikalpa*, Vol. 20, No. 1 (Jan.–March 1995), pp. 37–48.

Samuelson, Paul A. "Proof that Properly Anticipated Prices Fluctuate Randomly", *Industrial Management Review* (Spring 1965) pp. 41–49.

Samuelson, Paul A. "Stochastic Speculative Price", *Proc. Nat. Acd. Sci.*, 68 (February 1971), pp. 335–37.

Schwert, G.W. "Why Does Stock Market Volatility Change Over Time?", *Journal of Finance*, Vol. XLIV, No. 5 (December 1989), pp. 1115–1153.

Schwert. G.W. "Stock Market Volatility", *Financial Analysts Journal* (May–June 1990), pp. 23–34.

Sharpe, William F. "Capital Asset Prices: A Theory of Market Equilibrium and Conditions of Risk", *Journal of Finance*, 19 (September 1964), pp. 425–43.

Shiller, Robert J. "The Volatillity of Long-term Interest Rates and Expectation Models of the Term Structure", *Journal of Political Economy*, Vol. 87, No. 6, (1979), pp. 1191–1219.

Shiller, Robert J. "The Use of Volatility Measures in Assessing Market Efficiency", *Journal of Finance*, 36 (May 1981), pp. 291–304.

Shiller Robert, J. "Do Stock Prices Move too Much to be Justified by Subsequent Changes in Dividends?", *American Economic Review*, 71 (June 1981), pp, 421–36.

Shiller, R.J. "Stock Prices and Social Dynamics", *Brooking Papers on Economic Activity*, 2, (1984), pp. 457–498.

Shiller, Robert J. "Investor Behavior in the October 1987 Stock Market Crash: Survey Evidence", *NBER Working Paper*, No. 2446 (November 1987).

Shiller, Robert J. "The Probability of Gross Violations of a Present Value Variance Inequality", *Journal of Political Economy*, Vol. 96, No. 5, (1988), pp. 1089–1092.

Shiller, Robert J., Fumiko Kon-ya and Yoshiro Tsutsui. "Investor Behavior in the October 1987 Stock Market Crash: The Case of Japan," *Journal of the Japanese and International Economics*, 5, (1991), pp. 1–13.

Shiller, Robert J. and John Pound. "Survey Evidence on Diffusion of Interest and Information among Investors", *Journal of Economic Behavior and Organisation*, 12, (1989). pp. 47–66.

Shleifer, And rei and Lawrence H. Summers. "The Noise Trader Approach to Finance", *Journal of Economic Perspectives*, Vol. 4, No. 2 (Spring 1990), pp. 19–33.

Singh A. "Should Developing Countries Encourage Stock Markets?" *United Nations Conference on Trade and Development Review*, (1993), pp. 11–12.

Smith, Vernon L; Garry L. Suchanek; and Arlington W. Williams. "Bubbles, Crashes, and Endogenous Expectations in Experimental Spot Asset Markets", *Econometrica*, Vol. 56, No. 5 (September 1988), pp. 1119–1151.

Solnik, Bruna. "Stock Prices and Monetary Variables: The International Evidence", *Financial Analysts Journal* (March–April 1984), pp. 69–73.

Stiglitz, Joseph E. "The Allocation Role of the Stock Market: Pareto Optimality and Competition", *Journal of Finance*, Vol. XXXVI, No. 2 (May 1981), pp. 235–51.

Stiglitz, Joseph E. "Symposium on Bubbles", *Journal of Economic Perspectives*, Vol. 4, No. 2 (Spring 1990), pp. 13–18.

Stoll, Hans R. and Robert E. Whaley. "Program Trading and Expiration-Day Effects", *Financial Analysts Journal* (March–April 1987), pp. 16–28.

Summers, Lawrence H. "Does the Stock Market Rationally Reflect Fundamental Values?" *Journal of Finance*, Vol. XLI, No. 3 (July 1986), pp. 591–601.

Telser, Lester G. "A Theory of Speculation Relating Profitability and Stability", *Review of Economics and Statistics, 41 (August 1959), pp. 295–301.*

Tirole, Jean, "On the Possibility of Speculation Under Rational Expectations", *Econometrica*, Vol. 50 (September 1982), pp. 1163–81.

Tirole, Jean. "Asset Bubbles and Overlapping Generations", *Econometrica*, Vol. 53 (September 1986), pp. 1071–1100.

Trueman, Brett. "A Theory of Noise Trading in Securities Market", *Journal of Finance*, Vol. XLIII, No. 1 (March 1988), pp. 83–95.

Van Horne, J. "Of Financial Innovations and Excess", *Journal of Finance*, Vol. 40, No. 3 (July 1985), pp. 621–31.

Verrecchia, Robert E. "Consensus Beliefs, Information Acquisition and Market Information Efficiency", *American Economic Review*, Vol. 70, No. 5 (December 1980), pp. 874–83.

Verrecchia, Robert. E. "Information Acquisition in a Noisy Rational Expectations Economy", *Econometrica*, Vol. 50, No. 6 (November 1982), pp. 1415–1430.

West, Kenneth D. "Bubbles, Fads and Stock Price Volatility Tests: A Partial Evaluation", *Journal of Finance*, Vol. XLIII, No. 3 (July 1988), pp. 539–656.

Wheeler, Langdon, B. "The Oscillation of Systems: The Missing Link Between Price Volatility and Market Efficiency" *Financial Analysts Journal* (July–Aug. 1989), pp. 7–10.

Zeckhauser, R., J. Patel and D. Hendricks. "Nonrational Actors and Financial Market Behavior", *Theory and Decision* 31, (1991), pp. 257–287.

GOVERNMENT REPROTS AND OTHER PUBLICATIONS

Bombay Stock Exchange Official Directory
Business India
Calcutta Commercial Gazette and Investors Guide
Capital
Commerce
The Economic Times
India Today
Report of the High Powered Committee on Stock Exchange Reforms (1986)
Report on Currency and Finance, RBI
Reserve Bank of India Bulletins

INDEX

Animal Spirits, 54–55

Bear market, 4
Boom bust, 5
Bubble, 2, 16
    burst phenomenon, 3
    historical, 111
    new, 4
Bull market, 4

Capital gains tax, 107
Co-operative investment, 4
Corporate governance, 86

Deregulation
    international transaction, 91
    price, interest rate, 91
Distribution of wealth, 86

Efficient financial system, 87
Efficient market, 8, 11
    hypothesis, 1, 13
    model, 30, 43
Estimator
    classical, 113
    the Garman - klass 114
    'adjusted' high-low, 115
    high-low, 25

Fads, 54, 66, 84
Fair value, 6, 13
Financial
    crisis, 3
    institutions, 106
    sector reforms, 90

Fluctuation
    liberalisation, 93
    revisited, 46
    spikeless, 61
Fundamentals, 4, 17
    values, 3, 11

Insider trading, 99
Intrinsic
    worth, 6, 17
    value, 6

Liquidity, 99

Method
    a new estimation 115
    close to close standard
        deviation, 24, 113
    extreme value, 113
Market efficiency, 30, 66

Noise traders 184

Operational efficiency, 104
Outside finance, 100

Present value model, 14
Privatisation, 91
Psychology
    market, 2, 12
    investors, 15

Random price movement, 12
Rate of return, 26, 27, 38
Rational arbitrageurs, 14

Rational expectation theory, 1, 13
Regulatory environment, 105
Resource allocatiion, 85
Restructuring interest rate, 106
Rupee convertibility, 108

Savings mobilisation, 85
Security scam, 8, 45
Share mania, 3
Share trading velocity, 99, 109
Speculation, 98
Speculative
- activities, 3
- bubble, 11
- elements, 5
- episodes, 6
- fever, 3

Structural reforms, 103

Trend chasing investors, 6
- behaviour, 76

Value based rational investors, 76, 77
Variance inequality, 32, 35, 36, 67, 68
Volatility, 50
- defined, 23, 24
- information, 2
- in retrospect, 42
- in selected equity markets, 119
- monthly, 48
- market, 9
- price, 2
- 'spike', 52
- test with a revised detrended data series, 72